PRACTICAL PARALLEL PARENTING

RECLAIMING YOUR LIFE FROM CO-PARENT CONFLICT

BY R. SHELLY LOOMUS, JD, MSW

RoseDog Books
PITTSBURGH, PENNSYLVANIA 15238

RoseDog Books
585 Alpha Drive
Suite 103
Pittsburgh, PA 15238
Visit our website at *www.rosedogbookstore.com*

ISBN: 979-8-88812-390-4
eISBN: 979-8-88812-890-9

"A must read for anyone who is in the midst of a high conflict relationship with the other parent of their child/ren, after separation or divorce. Loomus provides a masterly cross-disciplinary approach to and of the legal system and human behavior, equipping the reader with a profound understanding of the dynamics in such families and how the court system responds. Most importantly, Loomus offers practical solutions of how to deal with the issue without compromising oneself. The book is readable and informative."

D. Berkovitz, PhD

———

"This is an excellent follow-up to Loomus' book *Winning Your High-Conflict Divorce*. The strategies provided should be followed by <u>all</u> divorced parents; they are insightful, practical, and invaluable. A must-read for parents struggling with custody battles and want to not only survive but thrive."

D. Smith, Ed.D., MBA, MA

———

Excellent insight about parenting challenges with real-life solutions.

L. Elassal, Esq.

———

In her compassionate, wise, and well-organized book, *Practical Parallel Parenting*, author R. Shelly Loomus uses her extensive background, as both a lawyer and social worker, in providing guidance to anyone raising children while going through a divorce. She shares her professional knowledge with warmth, grit and relatable stories and anecdotes. Her understanding of the legal process offers invaluable advice and clarity to the lay person during these often stressful and challenging times. She has great insight into family dynamics, offering practical solutions to sometimes overwhelming problems. She offers hope to the parent, so that their beloved children can grow up in a loving home with a positive environment. The reader is left not only with a guide, but with hope.

S. Rubenstein MSW, ACSW

Endorsements from Practical Parallel Parenting Seminar Participants

I wish this course were available to everyone. I think if I had this at the beginning I would not be where I am now.

Angela M.

—

Practical Parallel Parenting helped me understand the true nature of my divorce conflict and ways to disengage and build healthy boundaries.

Chris M.

—

The information presented was helpful and validated what was happening in our family.

Ivan S.

—

Practical Parallel Parenting matched up with my experiences and gave me strategies.

Denise B.

Client Endorsements

Shelly utilized vast real-world experiences along with clinical expertise to help guide me into a best possible co-parenting scenario. Her skills and support are priceless, and I owe her many thanks.

David V.

I reached out to Shelly on recommendation of a therapist who knows of her unique skillset, that she carries education for both counseling and as a lawyer, which makes her specially equipped to help those of us in post-divorce high conflict situations. She has used her knowledge as an attorney to help me navigate how to handle situations that have arisen with conflict in sharing costs, exchange of clothes, extra-curriculars, and medical expenses. She has used her knowledge as a counselor to help me understand the personality of my kids' dad, which for me has been the biggest help. ... She has also helped me in my grief of wanting something better for my kids in terms of a good coparenting relationship. We have to parallel parent. She has helped teach me how to do this. She is practical and her advice has helped me move through a very difficult time in life. I am so glad I found her when I did because I really needed someone just like Shelly.

Javana C.

When I needed an expert in family law, Shelly Loomus was an indispensable asset. Her knowledge and guidance helped me navigate the complex family court system and figure out how best to approach my case.

Jared B.

PRACTICAL PARALLEL PARENTING

RECLAIMING YOUR LIFE FROM CO-PARENT CONFLICT

To my husband and children, with all my love.

CONTENTS

INTRODUCTION

I endured a long and hostile divorce. It took me years to understand the dynamics of my relationship with my ex-husband. During that time, I changed my law practice from commercial litigation to family law, because my children were very young and I wanted to understand the system that oversaw and controlled our lives.

Together with my degree in clinical social work, I began coaching people on managing their high-conflict relationships with their former spouses. In addition to authoring a book on the subject: *Winning Your High Conflict Divorce: Strategies for Moms and Dads,* I facilitated workshops and spoke at seminars throughout my community.

My children are grown now, and I have identified three basic tenets that drive ongoing conflict between parents who no longer live together. The first is that one person in the relationship has a powerful need to perpetuate the conflict to enforce their truths. The second is that the Family Court System is concerned with parental rights, not with parenting. And the third is that the Family Court System and society consider co-parenting to be the ideal paradigm for divorced and separated parents.

If you share joint legal custody with your child's other parent, the laws in most states require you to make parenting decisions jointly. The efficacy of co-parenting can be measured on a continuum. On one end are the families you see on television and in the movies, where divorced or separated parents appear to be good friends. Somewhere in the middle are parents who do not get along but from time to time are able to make important parenting decisions together. And at the far end are parents who endure chronic co-parent conflict. While recognizing that the television ideal is not attainable, the family court system continues promoting that objective.

There always are and always will be disagreements, but if you are experiencing chronic conflict with your child's other parent, then that goal seems unreachable. When there is chronic co-parent conflict, talking does not help parents work together. One parent refuses to listen, and the other feels as if they are communicating with a brick wall. Most parenting issues remain unresolved because of vehement disagreements. Instead of co-parenting, parents are angry, stressed, and frustrated.

The Family Court System has little tolerance. Parenting concerns, such as whether a child should receive the HPV vaccine, seem minor when adjudicating child abuse and child neglect cases. Family Court Professionals believe that parents can be taught to co-parent and those who cannot are flawed.

These parents are not flawed. They are not selfish. And they do not lack the ability to negotiate and compromise. In fact, they regularly negotiate and compromise with family, friends, and co-workers. Once upon a time they probably negotiated and compromised with each other. These are parents who *believe* they are putting their children first. The problem is far more complicated than the Family Court System understands. There are complex reasons why every interaction leads to fighting, anxiety, and stress for millions of parents.

No one should have to live with chronic conflict. But co-parenting is not a concept that can be taught in a classroom. It is a **skill**, made exceedingly difficult when one parent is chronically combative. *Practical Parallel Parenting* provides a step-by-step guide for managing the conflict and changing the toxic dynamics between you and the other parent. Instead of being reactive, you become mindfully proactive. You will have a plan and a strategy. And you will feel confident negotiating. You will achieve the Family Court System ideal and co-parent while enjoying a life free of co-parent conflict.

CHAPTER ONE
HOW DID I GET HERE?

In any relationship, regardless of how good or bad your inter-actions are, it is important to understand who the other person really is. By now, you probably know that the person with whom you conceived a child is not who they appear to be. The person you first met appeared likeable and considerate. Perhaps when you met, they presented as Prince Charming or a Disney Princess. I refer to that as their Public Persona. In reality, however, many of them have a much darker side. You did not see it at first because they have a care-fully curated Public Persona. They are skilled at "reading the room" and understanding what is socially acceptable. They capture your at-tention by exhibiting a personality that is a calibrated balance of charm, strength, and vulnerability. Often, their courtships are swift because they have difficulty sustaining this Public Persona.

As your relationship progressed, you began seeing their true self. They approach the world in a vastly different way than you. Some-how, someone else is always wronging them. Eventually, *you* become the person who is "hurting" them. The conflict between the two of you may arise slowly, but once you begin fighting for custody and par-enting time, it quickly escalates. The other parent casts you in the role of Evil Oppressor and themselves as the Innocent Victim. You are now a Disney Villain.

Communication becomes impossible. When you try discussing an issue, they turn the topic to be about themself. Or they may:

- Deflect.
- Refuse to take responsibility and blame you instead.
- Project their own behavior onto you.
- Insult and disparage you.
- Gaslight you by denying your truths and insisting that their version of events is correct.

They may even threaten you physically. But they almost always threaten to take your child from you. It feels as if they are relentless, only stopping after you capitulate. Yet when you do, they find a new issue to complain about. I call this parent who always wants to fight a Chronically Combative Parent (CCP).

WHO IS THIS PERSON?

How does someone become a CCP? It starts from early childhood. This person may have been abused as a child. They might have been constantly belittled and criticized. Or they were severely punished for minor infractions. Their behavior was judged, and their feelings ignored. They grew up thinking they were never good enough. They feared being abandoned. Yet fear and weakness were not tolerated. Instead, they were required to appear brave and fearless. False bravado and insincere charm were rewarded. Anything less was derided.

Many children raised by strict parents are still loved and valued. While harsh at times, these parents successfully convey their love for their child, despite that child's weaknesses and challenges. But whatever childhood traumas a CCP experienced, at their core they do not believe they are lovable or worthy. Somehow their parents never displayed those feelings. Or the feelings were absent. Yet this child was still required to appear strong. Whatever self-doubts they had were hidden or denied so they could appear to be the person their parents expected them to be.

By adolescence, most children begin learning that people are not all good or all bad, and that someone can have both good and bad traits. They accept that in others and in themselves. A CCP's emotional growth, however, is stunted. They continue believing that people are either all good or all bad, including themselves. And because they cannot be 'all bad,' they must be 'all good.' In this regard, CCPs are binary thinkers.

This paradigm plays out in every aspect of a CCP's life. Every criticism or negative comment from a teacher, coach, or other authority figure suggesting they made a mistake, is interpreted as if the speaker is labeling them a 'bad person.' Being 'bad' is intolerable. It would negate everything they did to win their parents' approval. It would result in universal rejection.

Unable or unwilling to face this possibility, the CCP automatically rejects any and all negative messaging. No part can be true. Because, as a binary thinker, if one part of the criticism were true then all of it must be true, which would label them a 'bad person.' Thus, the CCP rejects the entire comment to reaffirm, in their own mind, that they are a 'good person.'

This process occurs repeatedly throughout the CCP's childhood and adolescence. Eventually, any negativity is automatically and instantaneously rejected. But it does not dissolve, because deep down, the CCP still worries they are unlovable. What happens to the criticism? I imagine a locked vault somewhere in the back of a CCP's brain. Inside are all those accusations, criticisms, and faults they have ever been accused of. The path to the box is so swift that an unwanted comment is instantly locked inside the vault and their subconsciousness revises history to support their truth, that they are a good person. Suppose, for example, the CCP calls you a derogatory name. Your respond by slapping them. The CCP will instantaneously forget that they spoke and only remember your slap. From that moment forward, they will see you as cruel and abusive. This is the world the CCP lives in. It is a vastly different world than yours.

The CCP has tremendous difficulty changing. Their denial and revision reflexes are too mighty. Examining a criticism or accusation would require self-reflection, which by now they are incapable of. Peaking inside the vault might unleash *all* the past negativity and in-validate their 'good person' narrative. Nor can a CCP empathize with others. Empathy requires hearing what another person says, which, in turn, requires them to see themselves from that person's point of view, a perspective that differs from their carefully cultivated narrative. Nor are they capable of problem-solving because, again, that requires hearing another person's point of view. Thus, a CCP becomes intrac-table and unwilling to compromise. They will fight to defend their narrative. And they will fight to fend off the possibility of losing. If there is no resolution, the CCP can never be wrong. Conflict, then, is essential to preserving the CCP's self-image.

Because you have joint legal custody and share parenting time with the CCP, you present the biggest threat. They want to possess their child unilaterally. They do not want to share their child, fearing you might reveal their faults and turn their child against them. Even teaching your child simple things, such as clearing their plate after dinner, may be in-terpreted as criticism if the CCP does not typically clear their own plate. Nor does the CCP want your opinion about parenting. Whatever you suggest is heard as you are accusing them of being incompetent. And they are envious if you have a good relationship with their child.

As the Villain in their life, and the other parent of their child, the CCP is most threatened by you and therefore highly motivated to prove that you are a bad person and a bad parent, and that they are a good person and a good parent. The CCP views every interaction with you through that lens. They fight you, not just to win the issue of the day, but to win the narrative. And they will continue fighting because if the fight never ends, no one can conclude that they are a bad parent.

WHAT IS CONFLICT?

Conflict is not just a disagreement. It triggers deep emotional responses because conflict is really about identity. Conflict is about the way a person thinks the world or the other person "should be." That perception is based on a person's upbringing and life experiences. Suppose a couple is offered an inexpensive weekend getaway at a five-star hotel if they listen to an hour speech about time-shares. They have no intention of buying but they agree. If you have ever been to one of these events, you know that the sellers are highly skilled at enticing you to buy. In my hypothetical scenario, the seller keeps the couple there for several hours and paints a picture of a lifestyle that is both affordable and luxurious. Ultimately, the couple purchases the time share. But the next day, one of them has buyer's-remorse. The other remains enthralled with this new image of their upwardly mobile lifestyle. The two begin to fight. Is the fight about the time-share itself? No, the fight is about their self-image as a married couple and the type of life they want or "should" have.

This was an obvious example, but it can be applied to most major fights. If a newly married couple fights about money, it is usually because they each have different ideas of how money *should* be spent and saved. If two divorced people with children marry, they may fight about how each speaks to the other's child. In this situation, they are fighting because each has a notion of how a blended family *should* function. Conflict, then, is about preserving how we believe the world *should* be and imposing that truth on the other.

When the issue is how you believe your child *should* be raised, and the relationship you *should* have with your child, challenges to that vision are particularly threatening. Your child is the most important person in your life. Unfortunately, the CCP feels even more threatened than the average person because not only is their relationship with their child threatened, but their 'truth' is threatened as well.

CCPs do love their newborn child. Many say with pride that the child looks just like them. Some even presume that their infant's and toddler's personality is just like theirs. In a sense, they see the child as their "mini-me." The CCP does not recognize a distinction between themself and their newborn child. Rather, they see that child as an extension of themself. And since their newborn is perfect, they must be too. Their baby's perfection reflects their own, and their own perfection is reflected in their baby.

When you and the CCP separate and your child is still young the CCP fears you will undermine their relationship. The possibility that their 'perfect replica' may turn against them, is unbearable. And should their child rebel during adolescence, then it is because you poisoned the child against them. The CCP, then, fights to maintain the ideal parent-child bond that existed when their child was an infant.

Challenging the CCP's narrative by calling out their faults to win custody, challenges that 'truth' about their identity. They want you to acknowledge and acquiesce to the perfect bond they share with their child. When you do not, when you tell the judge that the CCP *should* have done something different, they are enraged. Their singular objective is to convince the judge of their narrative. If the CCP wins a court battle they believe it was because the judge agreed with their narrative. They feel empowered. If the CCP loses a court battle, they are motivated to fight harder. The CCP, your child's other parent will always fight to convince the world that they are who they want to be.

HOW JUDGMENTS AND COURT ORDERS INANDVERTENTLY ENCOURAGE CONFLICT

Most Family Courts determine custody based on a *Best Interests of the Child* standard. The other parent (OP) quickly masters family court terminology and "talks the talk." They sincerely assert that they love their child and want to spend time with them. They claim that *they* are raising their child and sound sincere because they believe it. For example, even if they only bathed their child twice in four months, an OP will claim they bathe them regularly. They will interpret any situation where you oppose them as you are trying to take their child from them. If you are concerned about them taking your minor child out of the country because of the Covid Pandemic, for example, you are controlling and trying to deprive them of meaningful time with their child. In my first book I discuss courtroom strategies for responding to these narratives. In *this* book I focus on managing interactions with your child's OP outside of court. Unfortunately, the Family Court judgements and orders, while designed to help parents navigate custody, parenting time, and child support, are often exploited, and used against you.

The parenting plan is one example. Interpreting undefined words in their own favor is one way of using the parenting plan against you. One mother insisted that her "day" of parenting time was 24 hours but that the father's was only 12 hours. He had to get a court order stating that a day is, in fact, 24 hours. Creating chaos and confusion by not communicating travel plans is another. This was perpetrated by a father who lived in a different state than his children and had monthly visits with them. He refused to tell the mother when he was arriving or when he would return the children to her. Withholding information that is not specifically required is a third way for an OP to use the court ordered parenting plan as a tool against you. I know of a parent who planned to take his child to Disney World while school was still in session. He too refused to give the mother any information about when they would be leaving and how long they would be gone.

Most parenting plans allow for a change of the regular schedule to accommodate unexpected events. Some even specify those events. Others are silent. Regardless, to cooperate, you and the other parent may have occasionally agreed to changes in the schedule. Unfortunately, an OP's request for a deviation from the parenting plan is not always straightforward. Some OPs bundle multiple requests and make them interdependent. An example would be to request a schedule change for a particular weekend, but only if you agree to give them make-up time on a particular Tuesday and that you will pay for preschool childcare. But also, they might add, they will only do this if you agree to switch again on a Thursday two weeks from now so they can take advantage of the school break that begins on Friday. In exchange, they offer to give you the child on the Thursday of next year's spring break, but only if you reimburse them for the cost of the afterschool care that they paid on a Friday that they had given you in exchange for a Wednesday earlier that month. Do not trying understanding that request. The OP would have intentionally made it complicated. They are more interested in creating work for you as you try unpacking their request, than switching the parenting schedule. They also are interested in interacting with you as you try to accommodate them.

The OP manufactures this and other situations so that you must interact with them. You interact because you are trying to co-parent. They interact with you because, subconsciously, they know the conversation will devolve into a fight. And the fight affords them the opportunity to reinforce their narrative. If you had accommodated them, you made it unnecessarily difficult and was unreasonable. And if you do not accommodate them, you are a bad person.

An OP might also demand an answer from you immediately because of some, often contrived, emergency. An example would be that they need to make reservations or inform the people they would be traveling with. This type of request demands that you put aside your own plans to respond to the alleged emergency.

Reneging on agreements is a common way of generating conflict. Most parenting plans require that both parents agree on which extracurricular activities a child will participate in, especially if the activity falls on both parents' parenting time. I had a German client who wanted his son to learn to speak German. The mother agreed and the boy was enrolled in a class, but suddenly and without warning, she removed him. Of course, this angered the father but there was nothing he could do unless he filed a motion in court. If he did the mother would have likely claimed that their son hated the class. The father would have claimed that he enjoyed it. The presentation to the judge would become a "he-said-she-said" argument, something judges dislike. In such situations, the mother would likely win because a judge would prefer not forcing a child to take German lessons. Here, the mother emotionally injured the father by giving him hope that his son would learn German, and then ripping that hope away.

Setting you up to be the "bad guy" to the children is another strategy. The OP asks you for something, knowing it is a hot button for you and how you will respond. For example, they ask you, while your child is with them, if they can come to *your* house and get something that you purchased, such as their snow pants. You do not want to permit this because the OP has a history of failing to return other clothing you had purchased for your child. If you say no, however, the OP accuses you of denying your child the opportunity to go sledding and tells your child that they cannot participate because of you.

Child support orders provide another opportunity for an OP to antagonize you. These orders are not always clear about what expenses and what proportion each parent must pay, beyond those items listed. One mother worked full time but occasionally spent evenings entertaining at a local bar. Because this was "work," she wanted her ex-husband to pay for childcare, even though he was willing to watch the children himself on those nights. Another father initially agreed to share the cost of winter coats for his two children but then reneged and attacked the mother's character when she sought reimbursement. That same father also agreed to share the cost of their daughter's dance lessons, but later denied it. Just like the slap I mentioned earlier, the OP reflexively forgets what they said or did that generate your expectations. They resist looking back and refuse to look inward.

Court orders are supposed to provide structure and guidelines. Some are detailed, and some are not. That is because an attorney, or other family court professional, might recommend an imprecise plan thinking that you and the OP appear to be working together. But what they do not recognize is that one of the parents capitulated, as they often did during the relationship to 'keep the peace.' Regardless of whether the plan is detailed or vague, an OP who wants to fight will find ways to manipulate the language to create conflict and keep you engaged.

THE DIFFERENCE BETWEEN PARENTING RIGHTS AND PARENTING

The focus of the Family Court System is to protect parental rights. Parental rights establish your legal ability to raise your children. *How* you raise your children, your parenting choices, are personal. Thus, if you and the OP disagree about a parenting issue, the judge or another family court professional may decide for you, based on legal precedent. If there is no precedent, the issue may be decided based on the family court professional's own parenting ideology. I once heard a family court Referee ask a father why he wanted to see his children on a religious holiday when he could just see them later. There was little, if any, regard for the father's religion or parenting practices.

Most states use a "Best Interests of The Child" standard to determine custody and parenting time. The "Best Interests" standard is largely based on developmental theories grounded in Attachment Theory. Attachment Theory, at its core, postulates that a caretaker who provides a secure emotional foundation for a child fosters the child's feelings of confidence and self-worth.

Essentially, when an infant's or toddler's primary caretaker accurately and promptly respond to their needs, the child develops a core confidence that their needs will be met. The child learns that what they need and want is important. On the other hand, an infant or toddler who is left to cry and cry before they are finally fed or changed, is at risk for growing up insecure, fearful that they will not get what they need, or worse, that their needs and wants are unimportant. That child is less likely to take risks beyond their comfort zone than the securely attached child who knows deep in their bones that someone will always be there for them.

The "Best Interests of The Child" standard is a rudimentary assessment of how much caretaking each parent provides for their child. Some states, like Michigan, have a mandated list of factors the court considers. Other states provide little or no guidance. Regardless, decisions are made based on recommendations from Family Court Professionals (FCP) such as Magistrates or Referees, Therapists, or Guardian Ad Litems.

The initial concern of FCPs is whether the child's fundamental needs are being met:

- Does the child have food, clothing, and shelter?
- Is the child healthy?
- Is the child receiving an education?
- Is the child safe?

Issues such as whether the child learns to speak German or take dance lessons, and who pays, are parenting decisions and less important. According to the American Psychological Association, parenting involves three major goals:

1. Ensuring a child's health and safety.
2. Preparing a child for life as productive adults.
3. Transmitting cultural values.

The FCS focuses primarily on the first goal.

Preparing your child to be a productive adult and transmitting your values cannot be accomplished in a single lesson. It is a process. Productivity requires teaching your child a set of skills. Which skills you teach depends on how you define a productive adult. The same process applies to transmitting your cultural values. You must decide which values you will teach. The decisions you make regarding your child's education, choice of extracurricular activities, and religious upbringing, are all part of the process of raising your child. But they are minor concerns in the Family Court System whose focus is not on process but on *outcomes*. Has the child been educated? If so, whether the child took Chemistry or Advanced Chemistry in High School is not particularly relevant. To *you*, it might mean the difference between your child getting into the college of their choice or a lesser school, but to a Court that is coping with children being physically abused, it seems like a minor matter.

The risk of filing a legal Motion to further a parenting agenda that is being thwarted by the OP, is that the discussion quickly devolves into a he-said-she-said argument with no clarity about what really occurred. Suppose parents disagree about whether their teenage daughter should have elective surgery. The mother believes surgery will improve her self-esteem. The father disagrees, arguing that unnecessary surgery is too risky. The mother may now feel compelled to explain their history to the judge. She would want them to know that she thinks the father's refusal is really about the money because when they spoke, all he focused on was the cost. She might add that he never pays for their daughter's activities. Now the parents are arguing about what was or was not said during prior discussions on the topic. Hence, the "he-said-she-said" argument.

Judges dislike these types of hearings. They have little patience for reconstructing history. Imagine you and a friend have taken your toddlers to the local playground. While the children are in the sandbox you and your friend are catching up. Suddenly, a fight breaks out. Neither of you saw who started it. You ask what happened and both child blames the other. Does it matter who threw the first punch? At some point, it is likely that you and your friend will tell the children to either play nicely or you will take them home. Your neutrality seems fair to you, but to the child who was provoked and responded, being seen as an equal participant in the conflict feels like an injustice. That child may continue arguing that the other child was at fault. At some point, you or your friend might punish that child for failing to accept their parent's decision, and the play date will end.

Now consider the surgery issue from the Judge's perspective. The parents are arguing about who said and did what, but the legal issue is whether the father has a legal right to prevent the surgery. The answer is that he probably does because the surgery is elective. The father would win the motion. And like the child from the sandbox, the mother would feel that she suffered an injustice.

What if the issue was not elective surgery but the wish to send a child to band camp or on a church mission? What if one parent wants to administer medicine because they believe the child has ADHD but the other parent refuses? If a parent is willing to go to court over such issues, it is because they are trying to advance their goals for raising a productive adult or transmitting their cultural values. Losing impedes that parent's efforts to raise their child the way they want to.

Your loss is the OP's gain. The OP is frequently disingenuous in court. They say the right things to the judge, with sincerity, but their underlying (and often unconscious) motive is to perpetuate the conflict. What better way than to deny you what you think your child *should* have, even if that thing would benefit their child? In other words, the OP will sacrifice their child to hurt you.

This story is ancient. It was first told in Greek Mythology about a goddess named Medea. Medea was the goddess of magic and fertility. When she fell in love with Jason, leader of the Argonauts, she promised to help him obtain the Golden Fleece from her father, King Aeëtes of Colchis, on the condition that if he succeeded, he would take her with him and marry her. They married and had two sons.

But then Jason deserted Medea for the daughter of King Creon of Corinth, and she murdered their sons in revenge.

Obviously, denying a child the opportunity to go to band camp is not equivalent to murder, but providing these opportunities for your child is important to *you*. The OP knows how to hurt you. They have spent at least nine months studying you. And every interaction with you gives them more information to use against you. When they win a court battle, they feel empowered. When they lose, they are motivated to fight harder. But the Family Court System is not interested in how each of you parent, only that you do parent the child. Ideally, they want you to parent together. To co-parent. Only you know the uphill battle you face trying to do that with a person whose objective is to keep fighting you.

CHAPTER TWO
MANAGING THE CONFLICT

Everything we think is influenced by the paradigm or window through which we look at the world. This window is colored by our life experiences, culture, values, and beliefs. Conflict threatens our belief about the way the world "should" be. When you are having a conflict with another person, listen to your internal dialogue. You are probably telling yourself that the other person should agree with your perspective. Conflict is about proving your truths.

When someone powerful in your life challenges your truths, the ensuing conflict may become an existential threat. Your child's OP has power in your life. They have power to take your child during their parenting time, regardless of what you want. They have power to influence your child in good and bad ways. They have power to challenge how you are parenting your child. And underlying all of this is the knowledge that if they could, they would take your child from you permanently. I cannot imagine anything more frightening than the thought of losing a child.

Severe conflict triggers our "fight or flight" mode. It causes stress, anxiety, and fear. A person may be flooded with so much emotion they have difficulty thinking clearly. Living with chronic conflict has a negative impact on your health and your child's health. It changes sleep and eating patterns. It can cause an increase in headaches and other physical ailments. Living with the stress of chronic conflict can cause depression, feelings of helplessness, and sometimes feelings of hopelessness too.

But there is hope and you are not helpless. The three things you now understand about the OP is that:

1. They are wedded to their truths.
2. They will never hear you.
3. They want to keep you engaged in conflict.

It is the third point that gives *you* power. If keeping your attention is their objective, then you can choose to give it to them or not, and under what circumstances.

You cannot do this through conversation. They will not hear you and you cannot convince them of your truths. But you can change the dynamics of your interactions. Remember that much of the OP's behavior is reflexive. Lacking the ability or willingness to self-reflect, they proceed through life on autopilot. Think back on what you know about how the OP interacts with others. Are they quick to anger? Do they blame others? Do they avoid their responsibilities? The behavior patterns you see do not change. Unfortunately, you have become the focus of that negative attention.

The first step in managing the conflict is to change your own behavior. You can do this through Mindful Disengagement. By mindfully disengaging you establish boundaries between you and the OP. Once you are comfortable enforcing those boundaries, you can begin Mindful Engagement. Mindful Engagement empowers you to proactively decide *which* battles you will fight and how to strategically approach them.

MINDFUL DISENGAGEMENT

Mindful Disengagement involves accepting your reality and no longer thinking about how the OP "should" behave. You expect them to behave the way they always have. You accept that the OP does not and never will share your views about parenting. And while they will "talk the talk" of appropriate parenting and co-parenting, they are incapable or unwilling to "walk the walk."

Truly accepting your reality can be difficult. It defies your paradigm of how things *should* be. But it can also be liberating. You will no longer have that internal dialogue rallying against the OP's behavior and exhorting the way they *should* behave. You will approach interactions with a clear and realistic sense of what they really want and what they will do to get it.

The first step in Mindful Disengagement is to list the OP's strategies for keeping you engaged in conflict. As you do this, you should see patterns. OPs tend to have a finite range of behaviors. I have already mentioned some. These include:

- Diverting the conversation by blaming you, insulting you, gaslighting you, or casting themself as the victim.
- Creating chaos and confusion by adding multiple topics to the conversation or by failing to provide information.

There are others as well. One is to up the ante. One of my clients was a stay-at-home mom who wanted to spend one evening a month with friends. Her (soon to be) ex-husband refused, arguing that he did not want to be solely responsible for making dinner and putting their two young sons to bed after a long day at work. She defended herself by stating that parenting is also a job, but he argued that while he worked, she spent her days at the park with her "mom friends." Now on the defensive, she forgot to list her daily parenting responsibilities and instead conceded and agreed to prepare dinner before she left. But now he also wanted her to bathe the children. She agreed to that as well. Then he demanded she give him one weekend every fall to go hunting and one weekend every summer to go fishing. She agreed to that too. Thus, the price for one free evening a month was that she could not leave until she finished her chores, and that she accepts four days a year as the sole parent.

Another tactic is to use your concerns against you. One of my clients had far less parenting time than he wanted. During his mid-week visit, his daughter had after-school activities. Then she had homework and a bedtime routine. Knowing that their schedule was full and that my client never felt he had enough time with his daughter, the mother intentionally extended her goodnight telephone call to monopolize the child's time. She also listened in on his goodnight telephone calls when the daughter was at her house. Knowing how much my client wanted to develop a strong relationship with their child, the mother took actions to prevent that.

A third tactic is to distort your values. When you and the OP conceived, you probably thought you had similar ideas of how to raise your child. If the OP was still in the "honeymoon" phase of your relationship, they parroted your beliefs. But words can have different meanings or be interpreted differently. One teenager whose parents were divorced confided that he was confused about the meaning of Respect. In his father's house, respect meant doing everything his father demanded, without question. In his mother's house, respect was something entirely different. When he tried talking to his father about his confusion, he was accused of being a "momma's boy." The OP's automatic reaction was to lash out and insult his son. He would not allow his son to challenge his household rules. That the OP also hurt the boy's mother was an added benefit.

These are a few examples of OP tactics. When making your list, consider the process by which the OP generates conflict in your life. Do not focus on the subject matter. Focus on the OP's behavior and look for patterns. You may also occasionally revisit your list as the patterns become clearer. Once you have your list, familiarity will diminish your stress when the OP approaches you with an issue.

SOMETIMES IT IS BETTER NOT TO RESPOND

Sometimes reclaiming yourself involves refusing to respond to the OP's calls for your attention or refusing to respond on demand. Establishing healthy boundaries keeps you in control of your time and attention. When you are triggered, you have a choice. You can fight or flee. Choosing to metaphorically flee by not responding immediately to the OP's demand for your attention is sometimes the healthier choice. You would not drive your car while drunk because your senses are impaired, and you could not function properly. The same applies to interactions with the OP. If you are not functioning properly, it does not make sense to remain and engage.

"Flight" is not a negative choice. It can be helpful. By stepping back, you give yourself the opportunity to calm down and then analyze your situation and plan your strategic response. The OP often characterizes an issue as an emergency. By doing so they command your immediate attention. But true emergencies are rare, such as if your child is on the way to the hospital. By recognizing that the issue is not really an emergency, you free yourself to walk away and respond later. Their timetable is not your timetable.

For example, suppose you receive a call from the OP requesting an urgent schedule change because they suddenly have an opportunity to take your child to an exciting, new event but must by tickets now. Or they were invited to a party but need to RSVP immediately. In such situations, the urgency is contrived. They do not *need* to take your child to the event. They probably sat on the invitation until the last minute. The OP's "emergency" is due to their poor planning and now they are making it your problem. It is not.

The OP may also contrive the urgency of their request simply to destabilize you. They pressure you to set aside your own tasks and respond to their agenda immediately, without being afforded the proper time you need to consider your own schedule. Urgency promotes chaos and confusion. By generating it, the OP is in control of the situation. Stepping back and telling the OP that you will get back to them later, gives yourself the mental space you need to assuage the anxiety they created and calculate your response with a clear head.

Another benefit to leaving is that it shifts the balance of power. It sends the message that you will respond on *your* schedule. Expect the OP to resist, but you know their likely response. Will they start yelling? Will they prevent you from leaving? Will they accuse you of not caring for your child? In Chapter 3 I discuss how to manage those situations.

The remaining steps of Mindful Disengagement involve:

1. Enhancing your Emotional Intelligence to recognize immediately when the OP says or does something that triggers you.
2. Supporting yourself by taking care of yourself.
3. Creating a solid boundary by establishing a new paradigm: Parents, Incorporated.
4. Faking it 'till you make it.

STEP ONE:
ENHANCING YOUR EMOTIONAL INTELLIGENCE

Emotional Intelligence entails being conscious of your moment-to-moment emotional experiences. It asks you to focus on yourself and be sensitive and aware of your body's signals. It allows you to feel your anger, rage, or sadness. Your feelings are part of you, and you are entitled to experience them. Trying to suppress them will only cause them to spill out later in unproductive ways. Emotional Intelligence allows you to recognize when you *first* start feeling stress or anger.

Your body is often aware of a threat before your mind catches up. Some call this our "second sense." Our subconscious notices small nuances that our minds do not see because we are focused on the spoken or written word, and not on the minute changes in facial expression or word choice that warns of impending threat. It is important, then, to be more in tune with your body.

You can practice when you become upset by stopping to observe your breathing, heart rate, body temperature, and muscles. Are you breathing faster? Is your heart beating faster? Do you feel hotter or colder than normal? Are your muscles tense? Make time, either then or later, to identify that first moment your body started reacting. Then think about what happened. What triggered you?

Consider making a list of those triggers. The purpose is to identify *your* patterns. Are you triggered the moment the OP approaches you? Are you triggered by more specific behavior such as when they say something that is contrary to what they said earlier? When I was in college, I had a roommate who blatantly lied to me. I felt frustrated and even enraged because she was so obviously lying and refused to admit it. I learned that lies are one of my triggers. Think about your biggest fights with the OP. What did they do that enraged you? The reason for the fight is irrelevant here. Focus on their behavior. The goal is to identify the OP' behavior patterns that trigger you.

Once you have identified the behaviors that trigger you, try identifying the exact moment you are triggered. The purpose is this: if you are aware of the moment that you become upset, you can reclaim your equilibrium by walking away and taking time to strategically consider your response. You can also use that time to experience your pain and soothe yourself. That is Step Two of the process: Supporting Yourself.

STEP TWO:
SUPPORTING YOURSELF

It is essential to take care of yourself while living with chronic conflict. Conflicts tend to spiral out of control when people cannot think clearly and respond emotionally. People make poor decisions that they must later correct. Or they are unable to function effectively and fall behind in their work. Or they snap or lash out at others who are not the cause of their anxiety. Consider how much time is wasted trying to finish a task that you are unable to do because you are distracted and overwhelmed. Suppose it took you an extra fifteen minutes. What if you spent those fifteen minutes doing something to relax and refresh yourself? Once you are calmer you could complete the task with relative ease. Taking care of yourself saves you time overall. It also preserves your health.

To the best of your ability, take time every day for yourself. What do you enjoy doing to relax? Do you:

- Meditate?
- Exercise?
- Listen to music?
- Watch television?
- Talk to a friend?
- Take a bath or a hot shower?
- Take a nap?

Whatever it is, accept that you are entitled to a few moments for yourself. Do not worry that you are ignoring your child. The fifteen or twenty minutes you take will help the entire family. You will be less stressed. Therefore, your child will be less stressed. With less stress, everyone functions better.

Establishing a routine for taking care of yourself will help you manage the stressful times when you cannot slip away to meditate or take a walk. The knowledge that you will find time later will help you remain calm. Additionally, if you know you are about to embark on a stressful activity, whether it is confronting the OP or asking for a raise at work, taking a few minutes for yourself before that event will help you stay centered and focused.

Taking care of yourself is an important part of Mindful Disengagement because you are ejecting the OP from space in your head.

You are reclaiming yourself from the OP's demands, and from the demands of others.

STEP THREE:
THE NEW BOUNDARY OF PARENTS, INCORPORATED

The phrase "it takes two to tango," has always bothered me when describing an abusive or dysfunctional relationship. No one asks to be hurt. But I have determined that the phrase is really about Learned Habits. When one person is unpredictably volatile, the other might begin "walking on eggshells" to minimize provoking them. Or they might shut down, which, in turn, may cause the more volatile person to accuse them of failing to love them. There are many variations of these actions-reactions, but if they become Learned Responses, then in a way, both parties contribute to the dysfunction. That does not mean both are equally culpable. What it does mean, however, is that it is up to you to break your habits and change your own behavior.

People often talk about creating healthy boundaries but do not always explain the process. The process requires you to redefine the relationship. When you share a child with someone, regardless of your relationship with that person, you consider them a part of your personal life. The people in your personal life are family and friends. Although the OP is neither, because you share a child, they remain part of your personal realm.

But what if you moved them to the realm of co-worker? What if you thought of them as an annoying person who you frequently encounter and occasionally must work with, but they are neither friend nor family? Doesn't that more accurately describe your relationship with the OP?

Think of yourself as working at a company called **Parents, Incorporated**. At that job, you have a co-worker who continually tries to sabotage your work. You cannot complain to the boss (the judge) because the co-worker knows how to "Face Up" and has convinced your boss that they are a superb employee. You cannot quit. But you have options, depending on the situation.

If you encounter the difficult co-worker in the hallway, you would politely greet them and move on. Similarly, if you unexpectedly run into the OP, politely greet them, and move on.

If you were in a meeting with a coworker who is droning on about their personal life or complaining about your work, you would probably tune them out. Similarly, if the OP drones on, repeating the same point in different ways, you can tune them out as well. When your co-worker finally stops talking, you might ask them to send you an email summarizing their points and presenting a plan of action. You can ask the same of the OP.

If your co-worker ambushes you with a problem, your first thought might be: is the problem in your job description or in theirs? If it is in theirs, you would probably not agree to help. If it is also your problem, however, you might consider ways of addressing the issue without risking too much contact. A "divide and conquer" strategy, where each of you take on different responsibilities, would be optimal. Similarly, if the OP raises an issue that is not your problem, you do not need to help them solve it. But if the issue is something you also need to address, you can use the same "divide and conquer" strategy. In that way, you reduce contact, which in turn reduces opportunities to generate conflict.

Finally, just as it would be inappropriate for a co-worker to cold call you and expect you to drop everything to discuss a work issue, it is equally inappropriate for the OP to do the same. The appropriate method for seeking another's attention, whether it is a co-worker or an OP, is to message you and ask when a suitable time would be to talk.

By thinking of the OP as a co-worker that you must occasionally work with, you help yourself emotionally detach. Because you no longer consider them part of your inner circle of family and friends, their negative behavior should have less emotional impact. You may complain that they are annoying, but after venting you can focus your attention on the things that matter.

STEP FOUR:
FAKING IT 'TILL YOU MAKE IT

Mindful Disengagement might be difficult at first. You have had a relationship with the OP for at least nine months. Habits have formed. They know how to trigger you, and your reactions have been predictable. Changing your behavior takes time.

Fake It 'Till You Make It means pretending your job depends on you coping with that difficult co-worker. You would treat them politely but distantly. You would not spend any more mental energy thinking about them than necessary. You would accept their faults and deal with them as is. And most importantly, you would *pretend*.

It would be impolite to insult your co-worker. You would not tell your boss what you really think about them. You would be appropriately polite and keep your thoughts to yourself, as expected in the workplace. Treat the OP the same way. Pretend to be polite. Not only will you surprise the OP by behaving differently than they expected, but you reduce their opportunity to trigger you. That is because, to you, they are a simply an annoying co-worker at Parents, Incorporated.

MINDFUL ENGAGEMENT

Mindful Engagement means choosing if, when, and how, you might interact with the OP. You become proactive rather than reactive. The key is to know that you do not need to address every issue. When deciding, consider:

- Is the request merely 'noise?'
- Whose Problem Is It?
- Is the Issue Worth Fighting About?

Generating noise is destabilizing. Nonstop noise has been used to punish people, such as prisoners of war. The OP generates noise to destabilize you. The noise falls into four categories:

- Overly complicated requests.
- Urgent requests.
- Unnecessary information.
- Appeals to your compassion.
- Insufficient information.

The proposed schedule change I mentioned earlier is an example of an overcomplicated request. By tying multiple changes together and making them interdependent, the OP makes you work for them. Should you consider agreeing, you would have to unpack each request and the accompanying precondition before deciding if the change will work for you.

The same approach is often used with money. If you and the other parent owe each other money, perhaps for a child's costume or safety equipment, the OP may challenge your expenses. They might also condition reimbursing you on you paying them for some previously unknown and un-agreed upon expenses. These tactics change the conversation from pure math to questions of the legitimacy of the claim. This too overcomplicates the issue.

I had also mentioned the manufactured urgency of an OP request. By asking you to drop everything and address their issue, the OP has gained control over your time and the space in your head.

The most common topic of unnecessary information is the personal attack. An OP often feels entitled to make observations or judgments about you as a person or as a parent. Or they try to educate you about your child. They might say, for example, that "Brian is hurt because you wouldn't let me say goodnight to him," or that "You never think about Chandra's shyness." The common thread in both allegations is that you are hurting your child and they are coming to your child's rescue as their advocate. The insult is that it assumes you and your child do not communicate.

The OP may also feel entitled to "help" you become a better person or parent. One of my clients was "schooled" about the law by an ex who had no legal training. Another was constantly "educated" by the OP on how to be a better parent. In both situations, the OP was trying to elevate themselves over my clients by acting as if they were smarter and more knowledgeable. In the second situation, it took time for my client to recognize that the OP was not the "benevolent teacher" they pretended to be but was using the "education" to make demands. This had been hard to see at first because their initial impression of the OP was that they were kind and considerate. But first impressions are not based on reality. They are based on the OP's Public Persona, what they want you to see. Not who they really are.

Yet another example of unnecessary information is an email informing you of an event that has not yet occurred but which they know will upset you. One father sent his ex-wife an email saying that he was buying a house directly across the street from her. He never bought the house, but he did generate a great deal of agitation. Another mother emailed the father of her children saying that she, too, was purchasing a house in the same neighborhood. This email came with a list of rules, including a demand that should the children ride their bikes to his house on her parenting time, he was to immediately send them home. She never bought the house but again, she generated much consternation.

The OP may seek your attention by appealing to your compassion and empathy. You once cared and supported them. They enjoyed that attention and cultivated it by playing the victim to some third party's abuse so that you would become their advocate and rescuer. Even though the OP has cast you as the evil oppressor in their life, there are times when the OP would like to reboot that dynamic. They want your attention. One of my client's ex-husbands wrote, in the middle of an email about the children, that he was sad. This was an invitation for her to resume her nurturing role as former spouse. But she understood that they were no longer married, and it was not her place to make him feel better. That was a job for his current girlfriend. If the OP in your life occasionally tries to elicit your sympathy, remember that this vulnerable version is part of their cultivated Public Persona. Beneath that is a chronically combative parent.

Finally, by failing to provide sufficient information, such as when they will return your child or what their summer plans are, the OP generates noise by requiring you to ask, knowing that the conversation might result in an argument. Withholding essential information has always been a method used to control another person.

STRATEGIES FOR RESPONDING TO THE NOISE

Wading through the noise to find a genuine issue needing your attention, is tedious. Sometimes you must respond. Sometimes not. Regardless, you must still process the OP's missive. Take your time.

Regarding overly complicated requests, remember that if a person wants something from you, it is in their interest to make it easy for you. If the OP does not, it is a good indicator that what they are asking is not *really* what they want. Suppose the OP requests an overly complicated schedule change like the one I mentioned earlier. The numerous conditions they impose demonstrate that the schedule change is not their primary objective. If it was, they would be offering to give something up, not making demands. Additionally, their complicated request necessitates some form of negotiation, requiring you to communicate, which usually resulted in a fight. *That* is the goal. Remember, they fight to prove their narrative.

If you refuse their request, you reinforce their narrative that you are denying the children solely because you want to hurt them. This paradigm is familiar. You *know* the OP will deny your child to hurt you. If this sounds familiar, that is because the OP is **projecting,** which means to attribute their undesirable feelings or emotions to you.

If the request is too complicated, you *can* say no. Be prepared with a few simple responses such as:

- I'd like to, but we have a scheduling conflict. (You do not need to share your schedule with the other parent).
- That sounds great, it's a shame you didn't know about this earlier so we could have planned for it.
- We can coordinate for the next time this opportunity comes around, but please give me sufficient notice so we can adjust the schedule.
- I'm sorry but I really cannot change my schedule on that day. Perhaps another time.

These comments serve several purposes. First, by responding politely you are treating the OP as a co-worker. Second, by being polite and not emotional, the OP will not know if they agitated you. Third, by leaving open the possibility of a schedule change if the OP gives sufficient notice, you have informed the OP of your terms. It is now up to them to accept those conditions if they really do want something from you. And finally, should a judge ever read your response, you sound reasonable and willing to accommodate the OP at another time, thus negating the OP's claim that you are refusing because you do not want them to spend time with their child

A second option is to inform the OP that they have made things too complicated and ask them to clarify. If they continue convoluting their request, consider suggesting they prepare a Google or Excel Spreadsheet and color code their requests. If they do that, you know that their request is legitimate. If not and they complain, you know that what they are seeking is not worth their effort.

The third option is to agree to a one-to-one change that is clear and easy to achieve. Choose the option that works best for you. A benefit to this choice is that by occasionally agreeing to the OP's request, you will be unpredictable, thereby reducing the OP's confidence that they "know" you and know how to trigger you. But do not expect that the OP will honor your request for a schedule change because you agreed to this one. There are no bank accounts with the OP. You cannot build good will. They must continue viewing you as the 'bad person' to reinforce their desired reality.

Regarding the sudden and urgent request to take your child somewhere special, consider whether the activity is legitimately sudden and urgent (such as tickets to the World Series) or could have been addressed earlier. If the latter, recognize that you are being manipulated and let that inform your decision.

Should you refuse to accommodate the request, be prepared for the OP to enlist your child in a campaign to change your mind. This is a common tactic because you become the 'bad guy' if you deny your child. Being cast as the 'bad guy' by your child is uncomfortable. But do not succumb for that reason. The OP will always frame you in that light. Acquiescing will not change that. Second, although your child will be disappointed, remember that even children raised in an intact family cannot participate in every activity. They too will experience disappointment at times.

If you do say no, consider discussing the matter with your child. You know that the OP will blame you for causing their disappointment. It is important to acknowledge your child's feelings, especially when they are young and have not yet learned how to delay gratification. Very matter-of-factly and without embellishment, tell them that it is unfortunate their OP did not inform you of this opportunity earlier. Do not criticize your child's OP for their poor planning or organizational skills. They will not hear your words as much as they will hear that their parents are blaming each other, and your child will feel frustrated and even victimized. Instead, focus on skill-building. Even young children can understand that a person cannot do two things at once and that activities must be planned in advance. A simple lesson in organization will help your child later when they have complicated school and social activities and are still traveling between their parents' houses.

If you agree to the request, be mindful of your motives. Are you agreeing because this is not something worth fighting about? You may be making the right decision. Later in this Chapter I discuss how to evaluate your choice.

It is also possible you are agreeing because of 'divorce' or 'separation' guilt. Regardless of the prevalence of divorce in our society, there is still a stigma attached to it. You might capitulate to the OP because you feel guilty and want your child to experience as many fun activities as possible. That is okay. One of the benefits of having separated parents is that your child may enjoy more activities than they would if their parents were together.

Sometimes, it is okay to let your child participate even if you know that the OP feels they have one-upped you. In addition to being unpredictable (the OP having assumed you would say no), you are letting your child participate in a positive activity.

Alternatively, you may decide to take your child to the activity yourself. While your child will be happy, their OP will be angry at you for preempting their plans. They are likely to do the same to you in revenge. Try not to be upset. Many people, especially children, enjoy repeatedly watching the same interesting movie or participating in the same fun activity. If it is something your child enjoys, what is wrong with them experiencing it twice?

Regarding the unnecessary information that is clearly designed to upset you, it is important *not* to let the other parent know they have succeeded. If you respond with a series of counter arguments, such as why they should not buy a house near yours or that you are not stubborn and you know how to help your child with their math homework, you are rewarding them. You have informed them that they succeeded in upsetting you. Second, you have assisted them in their goal of perpetuating the conflict. And third, you are giving them information about what upsets you that they can use against you later.

Remember that the OP is not your friend and is not telling you things to help you avoid a conflict or improve yourself. They are telling you to reinforce their narrative. But sometimes they hit the mark. They may, for example, bring up an event where you were not at your best. Perhaps you yelled at them in public and still feel embarrassed. If you do find that there is some merit to the OP's accusations (and you will because they know what triggers you), talk to a real friend, a therapist, or a spiritual advisor. Do not talk about your personality or parenting style with the OP.

You should acknowledge the missive, however. It is not beneficial if the OP tells the court that you do not respond to their emails. Potential responses include:

- Thanks for letting me know.
- Thanks for sharing your thoughts.
- Thanks for the suggestion.
- I'm sorry you feel that way.
- That's not how I remember it.
- There is no point in rehashing the past.

Another option is to tell the OP that you are a different person now. One of my client's faced a scheduling conflict and arranged for her parents to look after the children. The father offered to take the children instead, claiming that the children never liked her parents. The mother responded by saying, "Things are different now." The father had no way to verify the veracity of her statement.

It will feel awkward if the OP tries eliciting your sympathy. You are a compassionate person who helps others in need. You have a history of supporting the OP. And yet, you have every right to be resentful. This tactic is clearly manipulative. Yet the OP may not realize that they are setting you up to once again be the bad guy. They may "genuinely" feel that they need and deserve your emotional support. Remember that this person has no capacity to see things from another's point of view. They do not know that they are being inappropriate. During my divorce, my ex-husband and I, and our children, were invited to a friend's wedding. We sat together. The ceremony was beautiful and touching, and my ex-husband took my hand.

At that moment he felt emotional and reached out to me because that is what he had done in the past. It did not occur to him that we were divorcing and that I had no interest in holding his hand. The irony that we were divorcing and that he wanted to hold my hand at a wedding, was lost on him.

Should your OP reach out to you for emotional support, gently but firmly say that you cannot help them. If you do not, and you try helping them, you remain enmeshed and impede your efforts to Mindfully Disengage.

Prepare for the OP to expresses surprise. They would have expected you to behave as you had in the past. That you did not will evoke their anger but do not try explaining the dynamics of what occurred. They will not understand. At most, remind them that you are no longer their partner

Finally, if the OP fails to provide necessary information, do your best to acquire that information elsewhere. If the OP does not tell you when your child's doctor's appointment is, for example, call the doctor directly. If the OP does not tell you what time they are collecting your child, go about your day. Do not sit at home waiting. Do not allow yourself to become their hostage. If you continue your scheduled activities, you will force the OP to deal with the consequences of their decision.

You can disregard much of the noise an OP generates. The challenge is to skim through to identify any genuine issues hidden within. A real issue is something that you *do* need to address. When deciding, first consider *whose problem is it?*

WHOSE PROBLEM IS IT?

If the OP presents you with an issue that does not concern you, you do not need to help them solve their problem. Often, the OP's problem concerns something that did or did not happen at their house. An example might be that your child refuses to go to sleep or do their homework at their house. If this is a mutual problem, if you face the same issue with your child at *your* home, you might consider brainstorming solutions together. But if the problem exists only at the OP's house, then it is their problem to solve. You cannot teach the OP to be a better parent or to build a better relationship with their child.

Another reason not to help the OP is because you do not know what is happening in their house. Perhaps they insist on watching television while your child is trying to study or sleep. Perhaps, if your child is young, they have not created a calm bedtime routine. You cannot ask these questions because then you will be accused of prying. Nor can you verify if the OP tells you that they already tried your suggestion and it failed.

The OP may try to enlist your aid by saying that their problem is your problem because of your shared parenting values. For example, if the OP is having difficulty getting your child to sleep at their house, they might remind you how important sleep is. Or if they are struggling to get your child to finish their homework, they may mention the importance of good study habits. Although you may agree, offering solutions will not help. When has the OP sought your advice and followed through? Have they ever said, "Thanks, I'll try that?" Or have they pushed back with reasons why your suggestion will not work?

The OP may also turn around and accuse you of interfering or sabotaging their relationship with your child. An OP frequently forgets (or represses) what they said or did that prompted your response. That they sought your advice is nothing compared to the hurt you now inflict by telling them how to parent. Additionally, while they may once have wanted your help, they may now resent that you might know better. It would be intolerable if *you*, the other parent of *their* child, knows how to parent that child better than they do.

Finally, the OP may try to enlist your help in solving their problem by accusing you of failing to co-parent. This accusation carries with it the threat that the Family Court System will punish you for not doing so. The OP might, for example, demand that you punish your child for something that your child did at their house. They may insist that the punishments be identical because "consistency is important." Here, they are again, "talking the talk." Were they in court, they would sincerely discuss the need for consistency and your refusal to cooperate with them. The judge would not be interested in hearing about the times that the OP refused to cooperate with you. But there are ways to respond that appear cooperative without becoming enmeshed in the OP's problems.

RESPONDING WHEN IT IS NOT YOUR PROBLEM

It is not your job to teach the OP how to be a better parent. If better parenting were truly their goal, the two of you would have been working together from the beginning.

One person imposing their will on another is not co-parenting. Thus, if the OP asks you to follow through with a punishment in your house for an infraction that occurred in their house, you are not obligated to agree. If you did not witness your child's infraction and did not participate in constructing a punishment, then you are merely a vehicle for the other parent to control what happens in your house.

In these situations, you can acknowledge the request without agreeing to it. Use statements such as:

- I'll think about it.
- I'm sure you can handle it.

Alternatively, you can agree to do as asked. The OP has no way of verifying whether you followed through.

If the problem is between the OP and your child, then respond by saying "I'm sure you can manage it" or "That's between you and our child. I cannot interfere." You can also remind the OP that there are plenty of online resources and books to help with common parenting issues. That way you appear to be supporting and helping the OP without getting involved.

That does not mean your child will not get enough sleep or their homework finished at their other parent's house. You are free to ask your child if they are having difficulty sleeping or studying at their OP's house. (Family Court Professionals cannot accuse you of inappropriate interference if the OP notified you of the problem). If your child does confide in you, help them solve their problem. Brainstorm solutions. Perhaps they can stay at school to complete their homework on the days they are schedule to be with their OP. Perhaps they can upload sounds composed to help people sleep onto their phone. Ultimately, your child will have to solve this problem. If the problem is with your child's OP, you can only be your child's coach. You cannot coach the OP.

MINDFULLY ENGAGING TO FURTHER YOUR PERSONAL PARENTING PLAN

Extricating yourself from disingenuous requests, or fleeing, helps you Mindfully Disengage. But there are times when fighting is necessary. The determination should not be random. It is important that your efforts having meaning. Creating a Personal Parenting Plan will help you gage whether an issue is worth fighting about.

You probably have some idea of who you want your child to be when they grow up. That person will be an amalgamation of your preferred characteristics so that they become that productive adult living by your cultural values. The list of potential outcomes is extensive. The first step is identifying which traits matter most. To start, think about who your child would ideally be once they reach adulthood. It is okay to fantasize. The purpose here is to list those traits and prioritize them. Aim for about ten characteristics.

Next is the reality check. Which of these characteristics could you reasonably expect your child to develop? Consider their strengths and weaknesses, their interests, and what *they* want out of life. If your child is young, that is probably not a question you should ask. Your final list will not be final. It will change over time as new experiences and information materializes. For now, though, prepare a list of the top five traits you can reasonably help your child develop.

The next part of developing a Personal Parenting Plan is to consider how you will help your child develop the characteristics on your list. For example, if your child has leadership potential and appears to be the leader of their social group, would becoming a captain at a sport they enjoy help them develop those skills? If your child is nurturing, then perhaps having them participate in their school's Peer Mentor program might be appropriate. Or if your child is fascinated by computers and loves building with Legos, then maybe having them join their school's Robotics Team would be beneficial. Hopefully, there are many opportunities available in your community.

The point of this exercise is not to create a single pathway to adulthood, but to guide you in selecting what is important to fight for. If your engineering minded child does not like group activities, then fighting the OP to agree that they join the Robotics team would not be a good choice. Your selections will change over time as your child matures. But at any moment in time, they will help *you* decide whether to engage with the OP.

I had a client who lived in a wealthy Jewish community. In that community, children were given lavish and expensive bar and bat mitzvah parties. The mother was frustrated because the OP refused to pay for the party unless she met his "conditions." His conditions were punitive and exacting. The OP had repeatedly humiliated this woman, both in private and in public. An elaborate party would show her community that she had not been defeated and would give her daughter a party that was equivalent to what her friends were enjoying. Yet the mother was repulsed at the prospect of acquiescing to the OP's demands. The decision was painfully difficult. But had the mother had a Personal Parenting Plan, she might have been able to separate her needs from her daughter's needs. How important was if for her daughter to have a party competitive with her peers? Or was it more important to show her daughter that she would not be bullied? Or was it more important to show her daughter that their lifestyle had not significantly changed since the divorce? Whether her goal for her daughter was socialization, emotional independence, or financial independence, a Personal Parenting Plan would have provided a framework for making the decision.

The Personal Parenting Plan would also reduce the OP's control. Their demands and behavior become one factor in the decision-making. The more crucial factor is what are *your* goals. With a Personal Parenting Plan, you make a more informed cost-benefit analysis in deciding to fight or flee.

Mindfully Disengaging restores your power. You are a parent, but you are also a person with needs and boundaries. Determine not to give the OP space in your head or the power to hijack your time, attention, and equilibrium. Give yourself permission to walk away. By Mindfully Engaging, you establish a framework for interacting with the OP. It is not your job to parent them, to respond to their emotional needs, or to help them become a better parent. Determine that the only issues requiring you to work with the OP are those involving your child that will further your Personal Parenting Plan.

CHAPTER THREE:
PARALLEL PARENTING BASICS

Parallel parenting gets its name from a similar concept in children's play. Young children who play in the same space but lack social skills, play parallel to each other. If they are in the same sandbox, they play next to one another, not with one another. Each child plays with their own toys and ignores the other. As children get older, they learn social skills and how to play together.

Metaphorically, you and the OP are fighting over the toys in the sandbox. Both of you have the necessary skills to "play together." You both cooperate with other people in your lives. The challenge is cooperating with each other.

If the 'cooperative' stage is equivalent to co-parenting, it is important to remember that co-parenting does not require you and the OP to make every parenting decision together. Other than the issues mentioned in your state's definition of joint legal custody (i.e., education, religion, medical care, childcare, and psychotherapy) there are no lists of what parenting issues you must decide together. Furthermore, we know that married couples do not jointly decide all parenting decisions. Decisions such as what a child eats for lunch or watches on television are not usually discussed. It follows that co-parenting cannot require separated parents to cooperate more than married parents.

The difference between co-parents and those who struggle with chronic conflict with the OP, is that co-parents have found a process for managing their disagreements. I know one former couple, both remarried, who bicker and disagree, but the four adults always rally when the children need help. Another woman married a divorced man with a young child. She and the child's mother were able to talk about the child's needs and participate in the child's life. A third woman I know also married a man with a young child. That girl was close to her father and resented her new stepmother. It was not until the child became an adult that she and the stepmother developed a relationship. But in the interim, the stepmother cultivated relationships with her many nieces, nephews, and godchildren.

Co-parents that manage their relationship, do so by analyzing the bigger picture. They do not have a formal Personal Parenting Plan, but they do have a sense of direction. They know when to stay in an argument, or when to give up and walk away. After presenting an issue and discussing it, each person independently decides what they want to do. You have the same power. You can mindfully choose to engage or disengage. You do not need to inform the OP of your choice. You *know* how the OP will react. You *know* that what they purport to want and what they really want are not the same. You have the advantage because you know how the OP plays their cards.

In any negotiation with the OP, there is the presenting issue and the real issue. Suppose the OP asks to take your child on a cruise with their extended family during winter vacation. They would need you to give up or swap some of your parenting time. The presenting issue is the cruise, and we can assume they would want to go on that vacation. But the deeper issues are that the OP wants to present an image to their extended family of *their* happy nuclear family with the OP at the helm. They also want their extended family to think they are strong and not subservient to you. If you have power over them, then their extended family would see them as weak or 'bad.' Thus, the real issue is, once again, proving their narrative.

How does the OP 'play their cards?' You know because you have written a list. You know if the OP will try to bully you, gaslight you, or insult you. But you also know that what they really want is your attention. They want to keep you engaged until you submit, so they can present to their extended family that they have conquered the evil you and that they are the good parent solely responsible for raising their happy, well adjusted, children.

It follows that if you communicate with them, you are ***rewarding*** them. Alternatively, if you mindfully choose to disengage, you are ***punishing*** them. Reward and Punishment are critical for managing the conflict. Think of Pavlov's Dog. Ivan Pavlov established the concept of "conditioning through association" by demonstrating that dogs could be conditioned to salivate at the sound of a bell if that sound were repeatedly presented when they were given food. Pavlov could not talk to the dogs and explain that they should be ready to eat at the sound of a bell. He had to train them. Although I do not want to equate the OP with the dog, the fact is that you cannot talk to the OP. They will never say "Oh, now I get it" and accept your point of view. The only way to change their behavior is to reward them when they treat you appropriately and respect your boundaries; and punish them by extricating yourself if they do not. In this way, you are developing a process for co-parenting.

There are some additional fundamental principles to bear in mind when negotiating with the OP. They are:

1. The only topic of conversation you need to discuss with the OP is your child. Everything else is noise.
2. If you need information about your child, go directly to the source. Do not, for example, ask the other parent for the date of Spring Break or whether your child did well on their test as school. That information is easily attainable from the school website or the teacher. Seeking information from a person who may be tempted to misguide you is not your best

choice. Find a work-around that does not involve the OP whenever possible.

3. Never use your child to transmit messages to and from the OP.

4. Preparation is essential. Consider this: if you like watching scary movies or riding roller coasters or other thrill rides, you mentally plan for it. When you purchase the ticket or agree to participate, you know you are going to experience that emotional upheaval. The same is true when you interact with the OP. You know their tactics. You know they will try to cause you emotional upheaval. By now it should be "old news." Former President Ronald Reagan famously said during his debate with presidential candidate Jimmy Carter, "There he goes again," reminding the audience that they have heard all this before and nothing new is being said. So have you. When choosing to interact with the OP, prepare for the likely attacks and deflections, and then steel yourself for the expected.

5. Always take notes on what you and the OP discussed and any agreements you reached.

Finally, even if you have decided that an issue is worth negotiating, the circumstances in which you do so may require you to extricate yourself. You should not continue discussing a topic with the OP if you are:

- Unprepared.
- Feel uncomfortable or unsafe.
- Feel pressured (unless there is a true emergency).
- Find yourself getting nowhere after a reasonable amount of time.

I have had many clients who tried for months to resolve an issue with their OP, but nothing was ever agreed upon. Sometimes the OP would delay responding. Other times they would suggest "starting over from a clean slate" which is a euphemism for disregarding all my client's concerns. Still other times they would change the terms. Or they would accuse my clients of being unfair or cruel. If you are negotiating with the OP and feeling frustrated, take a step back and ask yourself if the OP is acting in good faith. Do they really want to resolve the issue? The answer is probably no. People who negotiate in good faith manage to make some progress. If you are not making any progress after a reasonable amount of time, then it is time to stop negotiating.

THE NUTS AND BOLTS OF MANAGING COMMUNICATION WITH THE OP

Your interactions with the OP will occur face-to-face, through email, texting, or telephone calls. Face-to-Face communications are the most challenging because you have less time to think things through unless you have scheduled a meeting. Email on the other hand, affords you time to craft your responses. You will also interact with the OP within the family court system, whether that is in court or with a court appointed mediator, counselor, or parent coordinator.

Other than when you run into the OP unexpectedly, you should know what issue or issues they are likely to raise. (You will know because you will already have received at least one email on the subject). Take a moment to anticipate those issues and your response. Will you agree to discuss the issue immediately when asked? If so, consider the following:

1. What does the OP want?
2. What do you want?
3. How will you respond to each other?
4. What, if anything, are you willing to give up in exchange for that?

5.   Under what circumstances will you end the discussion?

Alternatively, you may decide that you want to wait and negotiate the issue another time. If so, you will need some ready responses to extricate yourself. The most effective is your cell phone. Whenever you encounter the OP, surreptitiously turn your cell phone to vibrate. If you need to get away, pretend someone is calling you. Answer the phone and after a moment of "conversation," tell the OP that the call is important and will take a while. Then walk away and continue "talking" until you are out of earshot. Not only does this provide you with a reason to leave, but if the OP becomes violent, you already have your phone and can easily dial 911.

FACE-TO-FACE INTERACTIONS

Face to face communications can be the most stressful. It helps to be mindful of the various times you may encounter the OP and how you will manage each situation. If the encounter is unexpected, for example, you would not have time to prepare. You may feel ambushed. Suppose you run into the OP at the grocery store or a restaurant. If so, all you need to do is politely say hello and move on. The OP may try taking advantage of the encounter to discuss an issue. If so, you have two options. The first is to shrug off their concern. A shrug is a nonverbal way of saying that the issue is not important and does not need your immediate attention. Alternatively, you can suggest they send you an email that you will look at later.

Be mindful if you are with other people. The OP may use that opportunity to say something nice to you. One of my client's OP publicly apologize for treating them badly during the divorce. Another OP publicly offered to pay their ex-spouse money they owed. Recognize that these are performances. If they were truly sorry or genuinely wanted to repay a debt, they would make amends without an audience and would not repeat the behavior. In this situation, a simple thank you should suffice. If they become angry because you did not "appreciate" their effort, then you know that they were insincere. A truly remorseful person would try harder to do the right thing.

What is the right thing? The socially appropriate manner to sincerely resolve an issue or make amends is to politely inform you that they would like to discuss something with you and then ask when a suitable time would be to meet. This approach respects you and your time. When the OP ambushes you, they are demanding that you discuss *their* issue on *their* time, regardless of your schedule or focus. By politely refusing, you change the dynamics. You create a boundary that lets the OP know that your time is your own and they are not entitled to your attention on demand.

The other three times you are likely to encounter the OP is:

1. When you are transferring your child between their parents' homes.
2. When you and the OP are attending a child's school or extracurricular activity.
3. When you schedule a meeting with the OP.

TRANSFERRING YOUR CHILD

The OP may believe that picking up or dropping off your child is an opportune time to discuss child related issues. It is not. Again, they are attempting to appropriate your time. If they are picking up a child, you probably have plans for how you want to spend your free time. Furthermore, they should be spending that time with their child because it is *their* parenting time. And if the OP is returning your child, you are entitled to be with them. The OP is not entitled to your attention simply because you are in the same location. Like any other adult or co-worker, they must request it.

In these situations, you may still choose to respond to the OP's concern. I suggest only doing so if you know *what* they are going to say and *what* you are willing or not willing to do. This will limit the conversation and avoid shortening your private time or parenting time. If you cannot resolve the matter in a few minutes, ask the OP to send you an email with their issue and proposed resolution. If you receive the email, you may choose to respond. If you do not receive one, you know that the issue was not really important to the OP. They were just trying to get your attention.

If you do not want to discuss any matters with the OP when transferring your child, have a few ready responses prepared. If you are home, consider:

- I'm in the middle of something and must get back to it.
- I have work to finish.
- I'm late for a meeting.
- I have an appointment.
- Someone is waiting for me or needs my help.
- I'm expecting a repair person, or I need to pick up something from a repair person.
- I have tickets and can't be late.

The OP is likely to challenge your statement. Know that you do not need to explain further. They are not entitled to know your schedule or how you spend your time.

Alternatively, you can give the OP a shrug, minimizing their concern.

Or you can acknowledge their issue but let them know you will discuss it later, by saying:

- I'll need to think about that.
- If you have suggestions, I'm happy to consider them. Why don't you send me an email?

Or you can say that you don't remember.

There are many more excuses available to avoid discussing substantive issues with the OP when you are not prepared. Be sure to rotate them, so you do not use the same excuse all the time. And do not feel remorseful for the harmless lie. If the OP was respectful, they would accept that you cannot talk at that moment. Instead, they are likely to complain or criticize you for not caring about your child. The harmless lie has a better chance of avoiding that abuse.

Lastly, if you are dropping your child off at the OP's home, say your goodbyes before leaving *your* house. That will allow you time to enjoy the moment without the OP hovering nearby. When you arrive at the OP's house, if your child is old enough, let them exit the car themselves. If not, unstrap your child from their car seat and quickly return to your car. Should the OP indicate they want to talk to you, partially roll down your window. Not only is your car window a physical barrier, but it again, indicates that you will not give the OP a large quantity of unscheduled time.

ENCOUNTERING THE OP AT A CHILD'S SCHOOL OR EXTRACURRICULAR ACTIVITY

The three times you might encounter the OP at a child's activity is when you arrive, at the event itself, or when you leave. If you drive to the event with a friend, then you reduce the OP's opportunity to ambush you. The same is true if you sit with a group of people. The OP may still approach you, but they are more likely to perform for your audience than initiate a conflict.

Still, the OP may catch you alone. If you suspect the OP may try confronting you at your child's event, you probably know what the issue is. Before leaving for the event, anticipate how you will respond. If the OP's issue is a complaint about you, simply shrug and walk away. If the OP wants to discuss a parenting issue and you do not, have some excuses ready. The strongest response is to remind the OP that you are there to support your child and will focus on the event and not on them. Again, leave your cell phone on silent so you can pretend to receive an "important" telephone call. Alternatively, you can say:

- I can't focus on that now.
- I need to use the restroom.
- I need to return to my seat.
- Someone (friend or child) is waiting for me.
- I need to get home immediately.
- I agree, let's talk about the details later.
- I hear your concerns, but I have some questions about your approach. We can talk about that later.

If you do decide to stop and discuss the OP's issue, try not to spend too much time doing so. Do not reward the OP for hijacking your time and preventing you from enjoying your child's activity. Not only will you be physically absent, but you may become mentally or emotionally distracted, and your child will notice.

The children's activity where you will most likely interact with the OP is at Curriculum Nights, School Orientations, and Parent-Teacher Conferences. The OP will insist on participating in any conversation you have with teachers, counselors, and principals. And they have the legal right to do so. Treat these situations as if you are at a Parents, Incorporated meeting with a consultant. The annoying co-worker is likely to do one of two things: dominate the conversation or listen to your questions and behave as if you are the spokesperson of your parenting team.

In the first scenario, you may not have time to ask your questions because the time allotted for these activities is limited. If so, tell the teacher, counselor, or principal that you have additional questions and will email later. The OP will want to know what questions you have. If they are minor or logistical, simply say that and move on. If the questions are substantive, tell the OP that you will include them in the email.

In the second scenario, the OP may ask follow-up questions to the teacher, counselor, or principal, or they may want to continue the discussion with you when the meeting ends. Take a moment to listen. Remember that sometimes the OP does understand your child's needs and may have some good insights. If the conversation is productive, reward the OP with your attention. If the conversation devolves into a personal attack, use one of you ready excuses to leave.

SCHEDULING A MEETING WITH THE OP

There may be times that you think it is appropriate to discuss a child related issue face-to-face with the OP. If so, meet in a public place. This will curb an OP's tendency to behave inappropriately. The OP does not want to look badly in front of strangers and therefore you can leverage this tendency to help maintain your boundaries. If you must leave, for example, the OP will be less inclined to grab your arm or yell at you than if you were meeting in private. Other ways to maintain your boundaries include:

- Limiting how long you meet. One hour should be enough.
- Arriving early to select a seat close to the door.
- Backing your car into the parking spot in case you need to leave quickly.
- Turning your cell phone onto vibrate and keeping it near you but out of sight of the OP.

Do not bring your child as they will distract both you and the OP.

Prior to the meeting, prepare an agenda. Since the issue or issues were known when you arranged the meeting, the agenda should not contain any surprises. But keep it short. No more than three issues or the conversation risks becoming convoluted as the OP jumps from one issue to the next and back again. The agenda will help because you can reference it to keep the OP focused.

The OP may struggle to remain attentive. They may raise new

issues or resort to personal attacks. Potential responses include:

- I hear that is a concern of yours, but it is not what we are discussing now.
- Let's talk about that another time.
- We are here to talk about our child, not me.
- If you disagree with this solution, what do you suggest?
- If you are not willing to talk about this, I'll go. I have other things to do.

Share the agenda with the OP, but not your personal notes. Prepare your personal notes before the meeting. They should contain a list of solutions you consider feasible, the list of the OP's proposed solutions, the list of solutions that may overlap, and the OP's remaining proposals. Do your best to focus the conversation on the solutions on which you might agree.

Suppose your teenage child's grades have fallen dramatically lately, and the OP wants to ground your child until their grades improve. Suppose you believe that is too harsh because your child is already resentful about their parents' divorce, and you fear that grounding them may exacerbate that resentment. You share that at the meeting and the OP reminds you that consistency is important and that if they ground your child, you must do the same. Now, there is no common ground. Rather than dive into the reasons you disagree, which may generate a conflict, your prepared response may be:

- Let's table that and see if we can find a solution that we both agree on.
- We are consistent in that we both believe grades are important. Our methods for implementing that need not be identical.

Then focus on the proposed solutions that have some common

ground. Perhaps both of you agree that your child needs an incentive, but neither of you want to give them money for grades. Perhaps you suggest that you take your child's phone while they do their homework and return it when they finish. If the OP agrees then the two of you will have successfully co-parented.

As always, keep your tone business-like and polite, as if you were at a meeting at Parents, Incorporated. Do not automatically reject all the OP's solutions. They may propose something you can work with. Alternatively, they may parrot your proposal and take credit as if was theirs. Try not to let your ego get in the way. Ultimately, it does not matter *who* resolves an important problem affecting your child.

I had a client whose ex-husband refused to reimburse her for their children's activities. I suggested a process for paying these expenses, which she, in turn, suggested to the OP. At first, he resisted. But then he made the same proposal to her as if it were his own. I advised her to agree because if he failed to follow through and they end up in court, she could tell the Judge that she agreed to *his* plan which he then failed to follow. She would appear to be co-parenting and he would appear to be resistant.

Only agree to a solution with which you are comfortable. Listen to your gut. If you need a quiet moment to think it through, excuse yourself and go to the restroom. Alternatively, you can complement the OP for their efforts and say that you like what is on the table but need time to think about it. Promise to get back to them within 24 hours.

Should the OP reject all your proposed solutions, invite them to suggest one that they have not previously presented. Wait quietly. Do not succumb to the temptation to fill the silence. The OP will likely be the first one to talk. In my experience, it is unlikely they will think of anything new and may become belligerent. They usually demonstrate that by insulting you.

If you find yourself becoming angry it is best to leave. Consider telling the OP that the environment is not conducive to resolving the issues and that you will try again at another time. This also establishes your boundary, telling them that if they fail to behave appropriately, they lose their opportunity to discuss issues face to face. If the OP responds in an emotionally or physically hostile manner, do not hesitate to make a scene. Let the people nearby know that you feel threatened. Their attention to the conflict should give you time to escape. Finally, if the OP abruptly leaves, recognize that they are trying to contain their own anger and let them go.

Do not worry that the issue remained unresolved. You can always negotiate through email or, if you are so inclined, at another meeting.

Take notes during the meeting or as soon as it is over. Send a confirming email about what was discussed and agreed upon or rejected. If the OP rejects the substance of your confirming email and argues about what was discussed, respond with a simple statement that this was what you took away from the meeting. In the unlikely event that you end up in court about this issue, your notes will also serve as evidence that you were trying to resolve the issue by co-parenting.

Lastly, make certain you perform any tasks you agreed to do. If the OP agreed to perform a specific task and does so, compliment them. As difficult as this may be, you are role modeling appropriate behavior and conditioning the OP to act accordingly. Finally, if the OP agreed to perform a task and does not, do it yourself. Their failure to act frees you to manage the matter as you see fit.

COMMUNICATING THROUGH EMAIL

Emails are the preferred means for negotiating parenting issues with the OP. Emails afford you time to understand what they are really asking. You can read them multiple times, think things through at your leisure, and then carefully craft your answer.

The first thing to know about emails, is that they are requests for your attention, not demands. Some emails are simply not worth responding to, and you have the power to decide when and how you will respond. If you suspect an incoming email will be filled with noise, remember that you need not open it immediately. Prepare by acknowledging to yourself that you are likely to be attacked and that the email may be filled with lies. Wait until you are ready, perhaps after you have had some time to take care of yourself. You will need to sift through the noise to locate any genuine issues they raise. If you find yourself getting angry and need to vent, hit reply, and delete the address. Then write away. Spill out everything you want to say. Just do not hit send.

Emails generally fall into four categories:

- Scheduling.
- Information.
- Money.
- Parenting.

SCHEDULING

I have already discussed one of the most common problems associated with scheduling changes: the interdependent multiple change request. The key point is to refrain from working *for* the OP. If they want you to accommodate them, their request should be simple and straight forward.

I discuss additional scheduling issues in a separate section below.

INFORMATION

Another common request from the OP is for information that they can attain elsewhere but prefer that you provide it. The OP might ask, for example, the dates of the next school break. Unless the OP has been good about reciprocating, you should tell them to get the information directly from the school. If they balk, suggest that it is in their interest to develop relationships with their child's school personnel. This is true and it would be good if they developed such relationships. Either they rise to the occasion and become a better parent, or they expose themselves for who they really are. But do not think that if you give the OP the information they ask for, you are engendering goodwill. There is no bank account with the OP, and again, you would be working for them.

MONEY

Money is almost always a source of conflict. Most involve payment of child related expenses. Unfortunately, child support orders can be difficult to understand, especially regarding medical insurance. If copays and uninsured medical expenses confuse you, a quick Google search should help. Be sure to add your state to your inquiry because not all states treat child support the same way.

Regarding child related expenses for things like extracurricular activities and school supplies/equipment/gear, and your child's college tuition, you should acknowledge to yourself that getting the OP to pay their fair share will always be an uphill battle. Unfortunately, you are unlikely to receive everything you are entitled to. Even wealthy OPs will avoid paying.

Some refuse simply because you asked. If you want something for your child they will automatically say no, even if your child wants it too. And they will find an excuse to justify themself and blame you. One parent told their child that they would not pay for a specific activity because they had paid for other activities, and it was now their other parent's responsibility. The problem was that this parent never provided an accounting of what they had paid in the past and so there was no way to verify their claim.

Some refuse because they believe they have already paid "too much." This is especially true if the OP is the payor of child support. They resent the monthly transfer of cash to you, believing that their money is wrongfully going to *you* and not being used for the children.

Some claim they cannot pay because they lack the funds. This may or may not be true. Be mindful that it is easy to judge another person's lifestyle from the outside, without knowing the details. The only way to get an accurate assessment of the OP's finances is to file a motion to modify child support. The risk, however, is that if the OP really is struggling financially, the result may be either a loss of money or you may end up paying more.

Some parents refuse to pay because they believe you are too extravagant. One divorced parent declined their ex-spouse's request to share the cost of a car for their son. This parent rejected the ex-spouse's claim that the son *needed* a car. While I never learned about the ex-spouse's lifestyle, I do know they had other children. I also know that if there are several children in a family, and both parents work, it is helpful for an older child to have a car so they can transport their younger siblings. I also know that this divorced parent did not consider their ex-spouse's needs when they refused to pay for the car.

If the OP is refusing to pay for a child related activity and you suspect the reason is because they do not want to give money to *you*, ask them to arrange paying their share directly to the activity provider. This might be more palatable to them, and has the added benefit of reducing your interactions with the OP.

The cost of school supplies, equipment, gear, and costumes can be substantial, and many of these items need to be purchased during a single shopping outing. If, after you purchased something for your child and the OP balks at sharing the cost, try a monthly billing system. Send an invoice, with copies of your receipts, each month. If the OP paid for any child related expense that month, deduct it. If they failed to pay the preceding month, include that amount. You can also try using a shareable document such as a Google spreadsheet, unless you fear the OP will use it improperly. Once again, you are treating the OP as a business relationship.

If at some point the amount the OP owes you is substantial, you can file a motion and hope to recover some of that money. Most states have a mechanism for handling unpaid child support, and you can usually find this information online.

Paying for your child's college education presents a whole new set of challenges. Ideally, include in your initial child support order a provision requiring both parents to contribute to the cost of their child's college education. It is important that this statement be specific. Do not use language such as "the parent will start saving for college," or "each parent will pay a portion of college expenses." It is better to include a percentage (such as 50%) and specify that payment will be for tuition, housing, living expenses, a computer, and required textbooks. While this list is specific, it may also generate conflict because a parent can argue that the choice of college is too expensive, or the child's apartment is too extravagant. However, because you have a court order requiring the parent to pay, you can file a motion asking the judge to enforce their order. You may end up in mediation, but the mediator can help you, your adult child, and the OP create a budget.

If you do not have a court order requiring the OP to help pay for your child's college education, there is not much you can do because your child is an adult, and the court no longer has jurisdiction or power to intervene. While I do not recommend belaboring the point, your child should know that you are sacrificing for their education and their OP is not.

Raising children is expensive. "Divorce" guilt sometimes results in poor financial decisions because parents want to assuage the hurt their child feels by purchasing things and activities for them. You can assuage your child's hurt feelings in other ways. Your child will feel worse if you impoverish yourself or are constantly fighting with the OP over money. Again, select things and activities that support your Personal Parenting Plan and recognize that collecting money from the OP will be painful. Consider what your emotional "breaking point" might be. If the battle over money becomes too stressful, then it may be time to stop seeking reimbursement. Your mental health is more important than chronic combat over tuition for soccer camp.

PARENTING

Emails about parenting fall into three categories:

- Personal attacks.
- Concern about a child.
- Criticism about something that allegedly happened in your home.

Personal attacks are noise that you should ignore. If you feel compelled to respond, simply say, "I'm sorry you feel that way." Do not engage in a conversation about your character.

If the OP raises a child related concern that you do not think is an issue, do not argue with them or try convincing them that they are wrong. The OP is likely to "dig their heels in" and the more you argue with them, the more inclined they are to believe their narrative. The OP believes everything that comes out of their mouth. If they say the grass is red, they will believe it is red and they will fight to convince you of their 'reality.'

Suppose the OP sends an email expressing concern that your child's friends are a bad influence. You have met the friends and do not agree. If you attempt to explain your reasoning, not only will they challenge you, but they may also prohibit your child from communicating with those friends. The more the OP convinces themself that they are correct, the freer they feel to take drastic actions. Instead of engendering all this drama, then, respond with a written "shrug." Remember that a shrug sends the message that you are not concerned. Therefore, your email should say the same thing; that you are not concerned. If the OP presses the issue, tell them to manage the matter themself. Chances are they will not do anything because deep down, the OP is insecure about their parenting, and you have neither validated their concern nor offered them the opportunity to self-validate by trying to convince you of their perspective. If they do act on their concern, your child will likely be angry because the OP's go-to solution is always a power-grab. Rather than having a thoughtful and respectful discussion with your child about their choice of friends, for example, the OP will impose a black-and-white, all-or-nothing rule. Your child will learn that their OP is authoritarian, while you will have met their friends and probably talked to your child about them.

You should address child related concerns that you agree are a problem. You have several options. The first is to punt the problem back to the OP. Respond with something to the effect of:

- I agree this needs to be addressed. What are your thoughts?

Should the OP suggest a solution that you disagree with, you can respond with a statement such as:

- While I appreciate your suggestion, I don't agree.
- Thank you but I can't support that plan.

Or you can say:

- That plan will not work for me. Can you suggest another?

This gives the OP one more chance to suggest a viable solution. If they cannot, the email conversation should stop. If the OP offers a partial solution, your negotiations can continue. But limit email exchanges to three per person unless you are making progress.

If the OP raises an issue that you agree with, limit the effort you spend trying to collaborate. Recognize that the chances of you convincing the OP to agree with you, are slim. But as co-parents, you must exert some effort to work together.

Suppose the OP claims that your child is fat and needs to diet. You agree but are concerned that the OP might begin monitoring everything your child eats and punish them when they make poor choices. To begin negotiations, offer an alternative solution such as therapy or having your child join Overeaters Anonymous. If the OP rejects your proposal, then, as with face-to-face negotiations, ask what *they* would propose. If the response is that your child just needs to "stop eating," the negotiation is over because the OP did not offer any plan of action. That would be a total of four emails. And since the OP dropped the ball, you and your child can now address the matter together, independent of the OP. If the OP complains, say something to the effect of "I'm sorry we couldn't work it out this time."

You can also remind them that they rejected your suggestion and failed to provide one of their own. In other words, they had their chance and now you are taking matters into your own hands.

Always be polite and stick with the facts. Do not editorialize. Remember that Family Court Professionals may read your emails. You want them to see that you are trying to work together to address a child related issue. That you and the OP did not agree is less relevant than demonstrating your efforts to co-parent.

Finally, should the OP offer a positive solution, suggesting for example that your child join a gym, you should support their effort by proceeding to negotiate logistics, such as timing and expenses. As long as the conversation remains productive, carry-on.

The OP's email may be to attack you about something that happened in your house, which they learned from your child. If so, deny it. Even if it is true, unless your child is in danger or your home is unsafe, the OP does not have a right to comment on what happens in your own home any more than you have a right to comment on what happens in theirs. A simple response such as, "You don't know what happens in my house," should shut down that line of discussion.

If the OP continues repeating your child's complaints, thank them for letting you know and respond with these types of comments:

- That is between me and our child.
- You have no say what happens in my house any more than I can tell you what to do in yours.

If the issue the OP raises is really *your* problem, then consider responding with a simple statement such as:

- Thank you for alerting me to this issue. I'll take care of it.

The *real* issue is what prompted your child to raise this concern with their OP. It is okay for your child to share what they did that day, such as playing video games or hanging out with friends, but if something upsets your child, they should speak to you directly. When your child's OP repeats something that your child said, check in with your child. First, explain that you are the person who can change things at home. The OP cannot because they do not live with you. Help your child understand what is okay to share, and what is private. This can be a difficult distinction for small children and may take a bit of practice. Second, listen to your child's complaint with an open mind. Remember that they live in two distinct homes which affords them an opportunity to compare home environments. Failing to respond by saying that "we do things differently here," or "that's what *we* do," will continue confusing them. Your child needs and deserves an age-appropriate explanation for why the rules and expectations differ in their two homes. And if your child tells you that something works better for them at the OP's house, do not reject it out of hand. Do not assist the OP's campaign to lure your child to "their side" by thinking that everything "over there" is "bad" if what they are doing works better for your child. There is nothing wrong with adopting it and customizing it for your own home.

Child related concerns about something that happened in the OP's house is the OP's problem to solve, not yours. As mentioned earlier, respond by "supporting" them. Say that you are "certain they can manage it," or that it is not your place "to interfere in their relationship with their child."

The biggest benefit of email is that you have time to strategize. You can step away. And sometimes you should step away. I believe that while your attention is elsewhere, your subconscious is working on the problem. And when you return to the email, you may have a solution you had not previously considered.

COMMUNICATING THROUGH TEXT MESSAGES

Texting is ideal for short discussions about logistics, such as what time your child needs to be ready, or where and when they need to be picked up. Do not use texting to address parenting or financial issues. It is not a communication vehicle that lends itself to serious concentration, and those issues are often complicated. Moreover, many people text on-the-go and are therefore less focused.

In addition to logistics, limit texting to issues that genuinely need immediate attention. People tend to read their text messages as soon as they receive them, whereas they may read an email later and let a telephone message go to voicemail. Text messages, then, are the best means of communication for genuinely urgent matters.

COMMUNICATING OVER THE TELEPHONE

There are several challenges with telephone conversations. The first is that it is difficult to think through your answers, especially if the OP catches you by surprise. If they cold-call you, you may be at work, repairing a busted pipe, out with friends, or busy doing the million tasks that you do every day. Additionally, an OP often uses the phone to destabilize you. Not only have they caught you unprepared, but they will also not allow you to think through your answers. They will fill your silence with more questions or commentary. They will speak faster and louder to elevate your tension. Flooded with adrenalin, it is hard to think clearly.

Second, unlike meeting face-to-face, the OP can call you from a private space. They choose the place and time and may select somewhere private where they cannot be overheard. This liberates them to attack you unreservedly.

As with email, you do not need to answer telephone calls immediately. Let them go to voicemail and listen to the message when you are ready. If the message is filled with noise, you do not need to answer. If the message presents a child-related issue that needs your attention but can be resolved through email, do so. You do not need to return the call.

If you choose to answer the OP's telephone call, be mindful of your breathing, heart rate, and any other indicators that you are getting stressed. Should the OP speak to you inappropriately, tell them that you are hanging up and will talk to them when they can speak respectfully. Then do so. This sets another boundary in your effort to teach them appropriate behavior.

It is possible that after you hang up, the OP will call back. One woman hung up while her ex-husband was yelling at her. He immediately called back, stated that they "got disconnected," and dove right back into his diatribe. He was oblivious to the impact of his behavior.

Her mistake was answering the phone call the second time.

Should the OP hang up on you, do not call back. Recognize that they are too agitated to talk and nothing productive can come from further communication at that time.

There may be an occasion where you feel the need to telephone the OP. If so, have an agenda. In the movie *The Big Easy*, the Anne Osborne character played by Ellen Barkin called Remy McSwain (played by Dennis Quaid), her love interest who she was also investigating for corruption, to explain why they could not have a romantic relationship. On her desk was a list of her talking points. The scene in this 1986 movie suggested that she was a nerd. Here in the 21st century, however, we recognize that people and relationships are complicated and that talking points help. Limit them to one or two matters, however. Spending more than 15 minutes talking to the OP on the telephone risks the conversation devolving into an argument. And if nothing else comes from the conversation, take comfort in the fact that you tried resolving a concern.

Finally, after every conversation with the OP, send an email briefly recording what you did or did not agree to, and what issues remain unresolved. Keep this with your records should you need it later.

COMMUNICATIONS BETWEEN YOU, THE OP, AND FAMILY COURT PROFESSIONALS

There are many Family Court Professionals (FCP) who may be involved in your case. These include Judges, Magistrates or Referees, Therapists and Counselors, Mediators, Guardian Ad Litems, and Parent Coordinators. Most Family Court Systems have a triage system. Judges adjudicate key issues such as custody and parenting time. Relatively minor parenting issues are first heard first by a Magistrate or Referee. If they cannot resolve the issue or if the parties disagree with their decision, the Judge decides. If the parents are at Court too often, the Judge might appoint a Mediator or Parent Coordinator to collaborate with them until they are less conflicted. And either a parent, or an FCP, might recommend counseling for a child or for the entire family.

It is common for the one or both parents to try triangulating their relationship with a FCP. Triangulation involves aligning that person with you and against the other person. Likeability matters. But some parents try too hard. Their efforts are obvious and therefore fail. Others are more skilled at creating alliances. And others are so uncomfortable that they shut down.

An OP can be charming. They are skilled at appearing sincere and credible. And they remember only what you did to hurt them. They never see what they did to cause you pain. Therefore, when the OP relates an event to a FCP they sincerely believe that what they are saying is the whole truth and that you are a bad parent.

It is unacceptable for FCPs to view you as the "bad parent." All parents make mistakes, but few are all bad in the way the OP renders you. Outside of the judicial system, FCPs know that parents are not all good and all bad. But when confronted with an isolated situation and two people accusing each other, it can be difficult not to judge.

The goal with any FCP is not to get them to like you. It is not to get them to validate your truths. It is not to get them to hate the OP. FCPs are not there to explore the long and complex history of your relationship with the OP. Unless a complaint is extremely egregious, the finger- pointing and blame become irrelevant. Rehashing the conflict that brought you to them becomes a "he-said-she-said" argument that will not benefit you. It is important to bear in mind that the FCP's mandate is to solve problems. Your goal is to get them to craft a solution with which you can live.

First impressions matter. You help yourself if you approach the meeting as if you were at Parent's Incorporated. Be professional and polite and focus on the issue, not the events that created the issue.

You will also benefit yourself if you make the FCP's job easier by arriving with a reasonable solution. Ideally, the solution requires both you and the OP to perform some tasks or refrain from performing a task. It should not be one-sided, although the task you would take on can require minimal effort. Not only does this make you appear reasonable, but should the OP fail at their task, the FCP will take note.

Providing a reasonable solution makes an FCP's job easier which will, in turn, make them appreciate you. I had a client who was upset when his young daughter's mother dropped her off without a coat, knowing that they were embarking on a trip to Alaska. This had been an ongoing problem. The mother rarely delivered their daughter with the appropriate clothing and the father understood this to be intentional; to anger him and make him spend more money unnecessarily. When speaking with the Guardian ad Litem (GAL) about this issue, however, the father did not inundate her with stories of all the times the mother failed to properly pack their daughter's clothing and schoolwork. Instead, he said that he was concerned about his daughter's organizational skills (or lack thereof) and made *one* request: to help him help his daughter manage her cell phone, her school backpack, and her clothing (coat, boots, etc.). The father presented a child centered solution to a problem which the GAL supported. The mother now had two choices. She could continue interfering with the transfer of the child's possessions, or she could help teach her daughter to manage her possessions herself, thereby gaining the approval of the GAL.

Another client's children completed their court-ordered therapy. Several months later, the young son made some disturbing comments at school. The school notified the father who immediately re-initiated therapy. The mother disagreed. She did not want her son taken to therapy every time he misbehaved, fearing he might start thinking something was wrong with himself. She was also concerned because she believed the therapist sided with the OP during the children's last therapy sessions. At the meeting the OP arranged, she let him speak first and express his concerns to the therapist. When he finished, she asked if she could speak. She then presented a statement she had prepared earlier. It included details of her earlier conversation with their son's teacher, who agreed that there was no cause for concern. It also included an alternative reason for his behavior. My client suggested that perhaps the boy had a bad morning and was simply acting out. The therapist agreed and suggested they do nothing unless the boy's behavior becomes a pattern. In the end, there was no therapy.

Note that this mother did not argue with the father. She did not even address him. Instead, she respectfully allowed him to speak and then addressed the therapist. She had prepared ahead of time and provided a rational alternative explanation supported by the teacher. Thus, she successfully kept the conversation focused on the son and not the adults. Additionally, the father had walked into the therapist's office emboldened by his past "successes" at "winning her" over. He felt confident the therapist would side with him. When she did not, the father had nothing to say. He was not prepared to discuss the issue. He was prepared to fight with the mother. The father felt defeated and did not pursue therapy for the son.

Alternatively, another client and her ex-husband met with their court appointed Parent Coordinator to discuss which extracurricular activities the children would participate in. Previously, the Parent Coordinator had ruled that the parents should enroll the children in only one activity per school semester and they would alternate selecting that activity. They were there because it had been the mother's turn to choose the activity. She did, but the father enrolled the children in a second activity. The mother went into the meeting believing the Parent Coordinator would support her because the father breached their agreement. Rather than talk about the children's exhaustion and poorer performance in school, however, she resorted to old patterns and complained about the father's duplicity. Her behavior reinforced his father's allegations that she was trying to alienate the children. The father was always charming to the Parent Coordinator, and she ended up ruling in his favor.

This father successfully triangulated the Parent Coordinator. A chronically combative parent will always paint you as a bad parent who wants to alienate them from their child. It is imperative that you do not allow that narrative to flourish. Remember that FCPs have access to your emails and text messages. Their impression of you is not solely from face-to-face meetings or courtroom presentations. Therefore, every communication between you and the OP must be crafted knowing that a FCP may review it. This is where Parents, Incorporated becomes critical. If you have mindfully disengaged, and you approach your interactions with the OP as if you were working with a troublesome co-worker, your communications will be focused and forward-facing.

When you *are* attacked, do not give it any credence. A simple shrug indicating that you have heard all this before and that the accusations are not true, will further the impression that you are not the evil and vindictive person the OP is trying to depict. Alternatively, you can offer a simple response such as:

- That's not how I remember it.
- That's not your business.

As difficult as it may be, try not to defend yourself. Unfortunately, people tend to view defensiveness as a sign of guilt. Instead, speak with confidence, even if you are uncertain that what you said or did was a good choice. For example, suppose the FCP asks you a question that will reflect badly on you, such as, "did you spank your child?" Answer with a simple "yes." Remember that parenting and parenting rights are not the same thing. Corporal punishment is frowned upon as a parenting method of discipline, but it is not legally prohibited. I am not advocating spanking your child, but I am using this as an example of something that a person would fear will reflected badly on them. The simple acknowledgement without a lengthy justification makes you appear confident of your parenting choices, (although it would also be appropriate to acknowledge that you may not have made the best choice) and makes it easier to redirect the conversation away from you back to the disputed issue you are there to resolve. You can say something such as, "Yes, I did that. I agree it may not have been the best choice, but that is not what we are here to talk about."

Finally, do not accept the OP's narrative. Instead, try reframing the narrative. The OP's narrative is *always* about you trying to take their child from them. Rather than explaining *why* you did something and how your decision was a reaction to something the OP said or did, present an alternative viewpoint. By providing the FCP with two versions of the same event, you are inviting them to choose which story sounds more reasonable. If you only defend your actions in the OP's narrative, the FCP has only one version of events to accept as truth.

One way is to refocus the topic from one event to the "global picture." Say, for example, the OP accuses you of alienating your child because you refused to let them call and say goodnight. Rather than defensively explain what happened on that night, you remind them and the FCP that the OP and your child talk almost every evening. If the OP accuses you of hurting your child by failing to help them with a specific issue, do not explain why you did not do that "one thing" the OP focused on. Instead, say something to the effect of "you know that we've been working on this problem since she was a toddler." When you take the conversation from a single event to an event within a series of positive actions, you reduce the chances of getting into a he-said-she-said argument. Instead, the conversation becomes about what has been happening overall and what is or is not working. It becomes a problem-solving conversation rather than a complaint.

Another way to change the narrative is to offer a perspective that is completely different from the OP's. I had a client whose OP accused him of failing to parent their daughter. By calmly stating that he and his new wife successfully parent the child, and by listing a few things they do such as purchasing school supplies and finding a new pediatrician, he presented facts that refuted the OP's allegations. The FCP then had to decide which "truth' to believe. Even if the FCP had flipped a coin to decide, my client would have had better results than had he said he purchased the school supplies because the mother sent their daughter to school with an empty backpack. Were that his statement, the FCP would hear another he-said-she-said argument. Both parents would be accusing the other of failing to parent. But by focusing on his positive actions, the FCP is less likely to accept the OP's accusations.

You can also reframe the narrative by presenting an alternate explanation that has nothing to do with the OP. Another client's ex-husband accused her of disparaging him and his new wife in front of the children. He accused her of making the children feel badly for liking the new wife. His new wife was outgoing whereas my client considered herself shy. When she picked up the kids from their father's house, for example, she did not linger to chit chat. Rather than accept the OP's narrative that she was intentionally cold so that the children would sense her distaste of their stepmother, she explained to their FCP that, as a single, working parent, her time was limited and precious. Standing around and making small talk with her ex-husband was not the way she preferred using her time. In this way, she turned the dialogue away from the accusation that she was being intentionally unpleasant, to the realities of who she was and how she lived.

In each of these stories, the facts were true but carefully curated. Every event in your life is a story. Sharing stories is complicated. You must choose which facts to present. If you were telling a story about taking your children to the Thanksgiving Parade and missing most of it because your youngest needed to use the bathroom, you would not include details about why you decided to attend the parade and where you decided to stand. You would instead talk about how far away the porta potty was and the long lines. You would select the facts that enhance your story. The same is true when you are with a FCP. The OP has one story. It is about how terribly you treat them. And every incident they bring up supports that story. You have many stories and many events that make up those stories. Choose the facts that will help you the most.

When meeting with an FCP, less is more. If you focus on solutions, the FCP has less information about you than if you try to get them to like you or if you defend yourself. It is harder for them to draw conclusions about you and therefore harder for the OP to triangulate the relationship. Do not assist the OP's efforts to define you. Instead, be polite, friendly, cooperative, and focused. If the FCP needs to define you, it is better for them to define you as a competent parent than as an emotional former partner.

MANAGING SCHEDULING CONFLICTS

The scheduling issues I have mention so far are in Chapter One: overly complicated requests to change the schedule, and requests designed to make you work for the OP. Additional sources of conflict include:

- Scheduling extracurricular activities.
- Scheduling invitations from family and friends.
- Scheduling medical issues.

SCHEDULING EXTRA CURRICULAR ACTIVITIES

It is rare for an activity to fall exclusively on one parent's parenting time. Parents must agree about which activity a child will participate in. I have witnessed many parents refuse to allow their child to participate in an extracurricular activity because:

- The other parent selected the activity.
- They were not consulted ahead of time.

- They do not want their child to participate in that activity. They have others in mind.
- They do not want the added burden of shuffling a child to and from an activity on their parenting time.
- They do not want to pay for the activity.

Regardless, courts support children's participation in extracurricular activities.

If the OP denies your child the opportunity to participate in an activity because you selected it, they are unlikely to say so. They will use one of the other excuses. If their rationale is that you failed to secure their approval ahead of time, they have a winning legal argument. It is necessary that you get their approval prior to enrollment. Most states require this. To circumvent the possibility that the OP will say no because you did not consult them, send them a short email with the relevant details (activity, location, schedule, price, and ancillary costs such as equipment) and ask for a reply within twenty-four hours. Include in your email a statement that if the OP fails to respond within that time frame, you will assume the answer is yes.

Often there is disagreement about which activity the child will participate in. The OP may claim that your child said they do not want to participate in a particular activity. This may be true if your child is young. Never having been exposed to an activity, their first reaction might be to say no. Alternatively, the OP may claim that your child wants to participate in a particular activity, but your child told you that they do not. This is not uncommon, as young children often try to please both parents by saying what they think that parent wants to hear.

One option is to expose your child to an activity on your parenting time to gage their interest. One of my client's sons wanted to play ice hockey. His mother (the parents were divorced) refused, fearing that he would be hurt. The father understood how much their son loved skating and wanted to help him develop athletic skills by participating in a team sport. Since hockey lessons and games were scheduled on both parent's parenting time, the father had two choices: deny his son the opportunity to play hockey or enroll him in a team knowing that the boy would only be able to participate half of the time. Instead, the father took a different approach. During a week of his summer parenting time, he signed his son up for hockey camp. He found other opportunities too and took his son to professional hockey games. The son continually told his mother how much he loved hockey and eventually she relented. In this way, the father circumvented the mother and provided for his son without any conflict. He also demonstrated to his son that he *heard* and *supported* him, and that is a powerful bond between parent and child.

A second option is to alternate selection. Each parent selects the activity every other season.

A third option is to enroll your child in the activity knowing that the OP may refuse to allow your child to participate on their time. That means your child will only participate on your time. This is unfair because they miss half of the activities. You can hope that the OP is sympathetic and eventually agrees to allow your child to participate on their time. However, the OP may interpret your choice as manipulative and refuse for that reason.

If the OP's reason for not agreeing to your child participating in a particular activity is because they do not want to do the extra driving, offer to drive yourself. The OP is not likely to agree because you would be with their child on their parenting time, so prepare for the rejection by having alternative options ready. One might be that someone from the OP's family or from yours could drive. Or a friend. Perhaps you could arrange a carpool. While this may seem like you are working for the OP, in fact you are working for your child. I would not recommend making this offer too often, though. The OP is likely to begin expecting you to continue arranging carpools for them.

If the OP refuses to pay for an activity, you have the choice to pay the entire cost yourself. The downside of this strategy, however, is that the OP may continue refusing to pay for activities, knowing that you will ultimately pay the entire bill yourself.

If the OP initially agrees to financially support an activity but later reneges, include the amount they owe in your monthly invoice.

Another source of conflict can be the location of the activity. The OP may select a location that is convenient to them but inconvenient to you because:

- They do not want to drive at all but will do so if the location of the activity is convenient for them.
- They do not want to spend their parenting time in the car.
- They want to inconvenience you.

I know one mother who enrolled her son in a soccer team that was miles in the opposite direction of the father's house. That same mother enrolled her son in a driver's education course that was located far from his high school. While the boy's peers walked to class after school, the father had to pick him up and drive him to another location. Another father insisted his son play soccer at a location directly between his and the mother's house. He claimed this was fair, but the reality was that the boy could play soccer *at* his school, with his school friends.

Unfortunately, there is not much you can do in these situations. While court is an option, it is not worth the cost. Additionally, filing a motion in court tells the other parent that they have succeeded in distressing you. Since that is one of their goals, by filing a motion you hand them a "win."

Do not complain to them either because that, too, gives them a "win." In these situations, accepting your reality is your best option. Do not dwell on how things "should" be. While you may be right, ruminating will only make you unhappier. And, depending on your child's age and maturity, they may understand that you are sacrificing unnecessary amounts of time to support them when their OP is in control. They may also question the OP's choice, recognizing that it is not child centered.

SCHEDULING INVITATIONS FROM FAMILY AND FRIENDS

Many Parenting Plans make exceptions from the regular parenting time schedule for events such as family weddings, funerals, and religious ceremonies. If not and you are invited to a special family event that occurs on the OP's parenting time, you will have to ask for a schedule change. Often, their agreement comes with conditions. One father would only allow the mother to take the children on a family vacation celebrating her parent's 50th anniversary if she gave him both equal parenting time in return *plus* make-up time for all the parenting days he intentionally missed. In such situations, a judge is likely to support you should you chose to go to court, as they accept that attendance at extended family celebrations is important.

If the OP has a special family event that falls on your parenting time, try accommodating them, asking for a simple, even swap. But do not think that reminding the OP of your generosity will cause them to offer you the same courtesy later. There is rarely a bank account. An OP tends to forget what they do not want to remember. However, you may gain leverage with the Judge, who will recognize that you did the right thing and reward you accordingly.

Parents have also been known to use family events to expand their own parenting time. One of my client's children were with their OP on Christmas Day. The children were supposed to return the next day and she made plans to celebrate the holiday with her parents. But when she picked the children up, they excitedly told her about a "really great Christmas party" that afternoon, that their dad wanted to take them to. This father was setting up my client to be the bad parent. If she refused, the children would be disappointed, and he could blame her for their missed opportunity. If she agreed, she would lose time with her children and her parents would be disappointed.

When I was about 8 years old, my grandmother took me and my sister to the zoo. On the way home I saw a carnival in the parking lot next to McDonalds. I asked my grandmother if we could go, and she said no. She said we had already been to the zoo. I never forgot. Not because my grandmother was wrong, but because she was not sympathetic to my sense of loss. Young children, and even some adults, want to do everything at once, and are disappointed when they cannot. But children *can* understand that people cannot be in two places at the same time. Still, the knowledge does not assuage their pain.

If you find yourself in a situation where your child's OP promised them something on your parenting time, you can say no without being the bad guy. After all, *you* were not the one who set them up. If you and their OP were co-parenting, you would have spoken to each other and agreed not to tell your child about the "really great Christmas party." Neither one of you would want to hurt your child by telling them about something they cannot do. But this is exactly what the OP did. Knowing there was a good chance you would say no, they hoped your child would be angry at you. If you said yes, they would have taken away some of your parenting time. Offering to take the children to the "really great Christmas party" was not child centered. It was cruel. So, acknowledge your child's disappointment and comfort them. It is real and they are entitled to their feelings.

Another scheduling issue involves social activities such as friends' birthday parties. If your child is invited to a friend's party that is scheduled on the OP's parenting time and the invitation was delivered to you, find a way to deliver it to them. Place it into your child's backpack. Scan the invitation and email it to the OP. Or simply send a text. It now becomes the OP's responsibility to RSVP and buy a present.

If the OP chooses not to participate or fails to RSVP, remember that their actions are not a reflection on you. Asking your child's OP to take your child to a party is more likely to result in a conflict than compliance. If your child complains to you, acknowledge their pain, and comfort them. Tell them you do not know why their OP made that choice. Do not add adjectives such as "irresponsible" or "uncaring." Your child will understand that their OP failed them without your prompting. Your acknowledgement that they suffered a loss is sufficient for them to understand that you are on their side.

SCHEDULING MEDICAL AND DENTAL APPOINTMENTS

Scheduling medical and dental appointments provides another opportunity for generating conflict. If the OP makes the appointment, they may schedule it during your parenting time, claiming it was the only time available. Or they may schedule the appointment at a time they know is inconvenient for you. If the OP schedules the appointment on your parenting time, you can always change it. Joint legal custody allows you to communicate with your child's medical providers. If the appointment is on the OP's parenting time, you are still legally allowed to attend. Do not complain to the OP or let them know that you struggled to adjust your schedule. Nor do you need to tell them you plan to attend. Simply show up. That will let them know that their obvious attempt to disturb you failed.

Another tactic OPs use is lying about the time or location of the appointment. One of my clients was court ordered to participate in family counseling. The mother immediately made an appointment and told him that the sessions would be on his parenting days. When he arrived, no one was there. She had lied and caused him to use up several hours of his parenting time in the car. Instead of confronting her, however, he called the therapist's office and verified the days and times of the counseling sessions. At the next appointment, the mother was not only surprised that he showed up, but also frustrated because she lost the opportunity to claim that he failed to attend the Court Ordered counseling sessions. Do not rely on the OP's scheduling information. Instead, call and verify.

Finally, if you are scheduling a medical appointment for your child, you may do so at whatever time is convenient for you, but do not schedule the appointment on the OP's time without consulting them. They will be the first to complain to the judge who will not be swayed by your argument that "they did it first."

MANAGING THE TRANSFER OF YOUR CHILD'S POSSESSIONS

Sadly, a chronically combative parents may use your child's possessions to hurt you. One of my clients and his son participated in Boy Scouts. My client had been a boy scout and loved participating in his son's scouting experiences. One day he gave his son badges that had belonged to the boy's grandfather. They were special to the boy, who kept them on the same carabiner as his other badges. The boy was working towards becoming a troop leader and needed the badges as proof of his accomplishments. One day during his mother's parenting time, the badges were "lost." My client doubted that his son lost them because they were so important to him, and he described his son as being very responsible. Both my client and his son looked everywhere for the badges, but they were never found. My client's son lost his opportunity to be the troop leader that year. Although he could never prove it, my client believes that the OP "lost" the badges intentionally. He believed that she took them because they included his father's badges, and she was willing to hurt their son so she could hurt him.

Unfortunately, you cannot enter the OP's house to look for your possessions. Asking the OP to return them merely satisfies their desire to annoy you. If you ask and get an excuse, thank them for the explanation. Your polite response to their obvious lie is a subtle rebuke without emotional drama.

When your child is young, you may have to accept that you will not get back everything you provide for them. OP's often fail to return your child's clothing or other personal possessions. Should you ask for their return, you will often hear an excuse, such as the item was lost, they cannot locate it, or they will not return it until you return the items *they* purchased. They may also accuse you of being more interested in money/possessions/things than your child's needs.

The solution is to be prepared. I had a client who picked up his children from their visit with their mother at a supervised visiting center, only to discover that they had no shoes. Apparently, when their mother dropped them off, she removed their shoes and took them home with her. Fortunately, this father kept extra shoes and clothing for his children in the back of his car. So did another of my clients. He also had a bag in his car that contained extra clothing for his child.

Replace missing items judiciously. When your child is capable of understanding, explain that you cannot keep replacing items that are lost at their OP's house. Do not blame them or the OP. Your statement is factual and fiscally responsible. It will teach your child the importance of keeping track of their possessions. Additionally, when your child returns to your home wearing clothing or carrying items purchased by the OP, make sure to return them. Consider washing the OP's clothes and have your child wear them the next time they go to the OP's house. This will teach your child how to care for other people's items. Your child will also learn that you cannot keep clothing that does not belong to you. And hopefully your child will notice the difference in how you care for the OP's belongings and how the OP cares for yours.

When your child is young and the OP fails to return items that you purchased, consider taking pictures of them and sending the pictures to the OP with a gentle reminder that these are the items that need to be returned. Alternatively, delay asking for their return until your child needs the item. For example, if the OP has your child's school backpack throughout the summer, wait until the day before school starts to ask for its return. If you do not get it, have your child carry their things to school in something else, such as a plastic bag. When your child complains, remind them that their backpack is at their OP's house. If they are old enough, they can speak directly to their OP who may return the item or give them a flimsy excuse for why they cannot. If the latter happens, your child sees which parent dropped the ball and failed to provide the thing they needed. Then take your child to the store and purchase a replacement backpack.

It is never too early to teach your child to be responsible for their possessions. Together, use a Sharpie to mark the labels of their clothes and possessions. Before they leave for their OP's house, show them the marks. Suggest that they keep these items in a separate pile. Help them learn how to do this by having them keep the items their OP purchased for them that are at your house, in a separate pile. Before they go to the OP's house, give them a bag to collect and carry the items in that pile. Additionally, when you talk to your child on the evening before they return to your home, remind them to look for the clothes with the marks and bring them back. If the OP tries keeping your child's items, they will have to explain to your child why they are keeping something that does not belong to them.

When your child is mature enough, spend a moment before they go to their OP's house reviewing what they might need. If they do not know, have them call the OP and ask what they will be doing and what clothing or other items they will need. Again, before they return, ask them if they remember what they brought with them that they should return. If things are not returned and are needed, comment that their OP must have forgotten to return them and acknowledge your child's dissatisfaction at not having something they needed. Do not editorialize. Simply state the facts. Your child will understand without prompting.

Another way an OP tries to control you and your child is to purchase outdated or ill-fitting clothing. This is not necessarily because they cannot afford better clothing. It is a way to force you to spend more money on your child's clothing. Should you complain, the OP might justify their actions by claiming that your child looks fine. These situations are particularly difficult because they may subject your child to negative comments from peers and adults.

The solution to this situation is challenging. If your child is young and does not notice that their wardrobe is vastly different than their peers, do not alert them. In this case, ignorance may be bliss. But if your child is more socially aware, or if they are being teased by their peers, you have two options. The first is to speak to the school counselor and ask them to speak to the OP without mentioning you. Since your child's OP wants the approval of third parties, they may respond positively to a recommendation to purchase more age-appropriate clothing. The second option is to suggest that your child speak to their OP. Help them find the right words to advocate for themself and then have them practice with you. Ask them how their OP is likely to respond and encourage them to produce answers. Or suggest they ask the OP for an allowance or an opportunity to earn money so they can buy their own clothes.

Another problem is if the OP always returns your child in the same, dirty clothes they wore when they left your house three days earlier. This happened to one of my clients. Her ex-spouse returned their daughter in the same clothes she wore when she went to his house three days earlier. He did not even have her change her underwear. She returned filthy. Her solution was to put a plastic bag with some extra pairs of underwear in the child's backpack. As soon as the daughter was old enough, the mother taught her how to use the washing machine and dryer, with the hope that the father would allow her to wash her clothes at his house.

Yet another OP tactic is to ask to borrow something from your house that your child needs. They either call you in the presence of your child, or have your child ask. This is a win-win for them. If you give them the item, they have taken something from you. If you do not, they can tell your child that it is *your* fault they do not have what they need. In this situation, consider whether the item is something your child needs or wants. If they want a particular pair of shoes from your house, for example, they already have the shoes they wore to the OP's house. If those shoes are not appropriate for the occasion, consider whether those shoes were something the OP should have purchased, or your child should have packed when they left for the OP's home. If so, at an appropriate time explain in a matter of fact, non-accusatory manner, that the shoes were their OP's or their own responsibility. If, however, neither of those situations apply, or the item is something your child does need, then you should give it to them.

Yet another OP tactic is to place unreasonable demands on the use of items you purchased for your child. These usually involve cell phones which the OP restricts for the purpose of limiting your communication with your child when they are with the OP. One father hid his child's cellphone (purchased by the mother) during his parenting time. Another parent refused to allow their child to communicate with their OP on the cell phone they purchased. A third prohibited the child from bringing their cell phone into their house. In these situations, consider purchasing an inexpensive second phone for your child. One they can hide from their OP. Instruct them that they should only use this for emergencies.

Transferring extracurricular uniforms, costumes, and equipment creates another problem if your child transfers between parents' houses at someplace other than home. Lugging all their supplies, plus their computer and books, is cumbersome and requires a place to store things while at school. Their lockers are often too small. If the activity is affiliated with school, storage space is usually provided. Some schools may also allow students to store their equipment for non-school related activities, but many do not. In that case, the sending parent is usually responsible for ensuring these items return with the child. If that is you and your child is going to school on the bus but cannot carry all of their things, leave them on the side of your house for the OP to collect. Alternatively, you can drive your child to school, ask that the items remain in the reception area until the OP retrieves them. Either you or your child can text the OP to let them know where the items are temporarily stored. Ideally, the OP will employ the same arrangement. If not, and your child returns home without something they need, help your child retrieve it from their OP if convenient, but do not comment. Your maturing child will understand which parent failed to consider their needs.

Consider saving money to buy a car for your child as soon as they turn sixteen. Having their own car gives them a place to store their school and extracurricular activities and transport them between houses and school. It also enables your child to navigate between their parents' houses more independently. This in turn gives your child more control over their relationship with both parents.

Some parents may balk at these strategies because they rightly believe it is the OP's responsibility. If you feel uncomfortable, remember that you are not the parent that created the problem. Were the OP willing to return items at your request, your child would not be in this situation. Unfortunately, the OP's machinations require your child to mature faster than others. However, even a five-year-old child who goes to camp has labels on their clothing, so they know what belongs to them. The difference is that at camp, the counselors help the child recover their items, whereas the OP is working against them. This is a difficult lesson for a child to learn, but it is your child's reality and as much as you want to protect them, they *will* learn who their OP really is. Knowing and accepting that reality will help them manage their relationship with their OP.

CHAPTER FOUR:
PRACTICAL PARALLEL PARENTING AT HOME

Your relationship with the OP, and your child's relationship with that parent, are not the same. While you may observe familiar behavior patterns that you believe will hurt your child, your child experiences them differently. Children are biologically wired to want their parent's love and approval. They will tolerate a lot to get that. Furthermore, until children go out into the world and observe other families and parent-child relationships, they will assume that their experiences are normal. One advantage of living separately from your child's OP is that you offer your child a clear distinction between lifestyles and values. Nonetheless, you cannot presume to know exactly what happens when your child is with their OP, and you cannot presume that your child will respond the same way you might have.

Another thing to remember is that your child is composed of 50% of each of their parents. When you criticize their OP, they may internalize what you are saying and think you are implicating them as well. Or they may internalize your feelings as their own. Some children align with the OP out of a sense of loyalty. Still others check out and detach from both parents. None of these are healthy responses. They prevent your child from seeing their parents through their own eyes.

Excessive criticism and disparagement of another parent, then, can arrest your child's natural development and hamper their ability to develop independent relationships with you and their OP. It may take years of therapy to recover.

Eventually we all learn that our parents are fallible. That they too have strengths and weaknesses. And most learn to accept them as they are and still love their parents. Children with chronically combative parents learn about that parent's weaknesses and challenges earlier than most. Your job is not to highlight the OP's faults, but to help your child develop the skills to navigate them. It is your child's choice, when they become adults, if and how they will relate to the OP.

The court prohibits you from disparaging their other parent. You are not your child's friend. A friend can agree that their parent is a "bastard," but you cannot. If your child calls their OP an inappropriate name, validate their feelings of anger, but not their adjectives. Thus, if your child says that "mom is a bitch," you can ask what caused them to feel that way, agree that whatever happened was hurtful and unfair, but avoid saying that you agree that their "mom is a bitch." It is always possible that your child will inadvertently tell their OP or a Family Court Professional what you said about their mother, and no one will hear that you were supporting your child. Family Court Professionals will tell you, instead, that you should neither tolerate nor use such language when talking about your child's OP.

Many adults successfully manage their relationships with their chronically combative parents. They established healthy boundaries and are aware when their OP attempts to manipulate them. Eventually, the OP learns that if they want a relationship with their adult child, they must restrain themselves. There are other adults who choose not to see their OP without rejecting the possibility that they may develop a relationship sometime in the future. And others choose never to see their OP again. What relationship your adult child chooses to have with their OP is theirs to make. Trying to influence them may result in your child choosing to distance themselves from you. But helping them cope with their difficult OP, teaching them the skills they need to succeed in *their* life, will cement your relationship. A child who knows that you are there for *them* and not driven by your own agenda, will always love and appreciate you.

You cannot teach the OP to be a better parent. You cannot rescue them from the consequences of their parenting mistakes. They will not listen, and they will resent you. Explaining how to pack your child's lunch or what your child prefers eating is a double-edges sword. Even if the OP appears receptive, they will also be angry because, by advising them, you put yourself in the superior position. One divorced father demanded that he be the parent who provided his child's emergency bundle. This family lived in an area prone to earthquakes and it was the school's policy for every child to have food, a blanket, a picture of their family and a note from their parents. The mother had been providing this for years until the father insisted it was his turn. The mother acquiesced, but the child never received their emergency bundle. The father wanted the *right* and *recognition* of performing the task but did not really want to do it. Had the mother discussed her concern that he might not follow through, a big conflict would have ensued. Instead, she let him fail and then later brought the earthquake-pack to their child's school. The father never followed up with the school to verify that the child had their earthquake-pack. It did not matter to him. What mattered was that he had the same "right" as the mother.

Suppose the first day of the school year falls on the OP's parenting time. Earlier, you received a list of supplies your child needs. The OP should have received this list too. It was their responsibility to put themselves on the school mailing list. Suppose they did not and are now asking you for a copy of the list. Giving it to them would be the easy thing to do. You would be rescuing them, but presumably they would purchase the necessary items. One problem, however, is that the OP may begin relying on you to provide for them, knowing that you will do so to help your child have what they need. You may end up working for the OP, but they will not be grateful. Instead, they will resent you because their dependence defies their narrative that they are a competent parent.

On the other hand, if you do not give them the school list they will be outraged and accuse you of being mean spirited or selfish. Still, you are not in a lose-lose situation. If you sent them the URL to the supply list, you would be helping them become a better parent, they would now have the list to purchase the necessary items, but you would not be working for them. Nor would you generate a conflict by refusing their request.

Suppose this father never purchased the school supplies, even after the mother sent the URL. Suppose the mother quietly purchased the items and delivered them to the school. Do you think this father would follow up to make certain the child had what they needed? The answer is no. If the father were really interested in ensuring the child had what they needed, the father could have located the school list and purchased the items. Instead, he reached out to the mother because he *needs* to continue their relationship until he unequivocally proves that he is a competent and *better* parent.

In both scenarios, the mother did not teach the father how to be a better parent. There was no conversation. Nor did she rescue him. Neither father knew that their child received their school supplies. Once the event ended, they forgot about it. But the crucial point is that both children got what they needed.

There are some parents who learn from their mistakes. OPs are extremely sensitive to public opinion. When one young boy was in elementary school, his mother failed to deliver Birthday treats to his class. For two years the stepmother delivered the treats. The third year, the boy's mother did it. I call this **Better Parenting Through Competition**. In the previous scenarios, had either father walked into school to see the new classroom and meet the teacher, they might have seen the other parents delivering school supplies and then, wanting to appear to be a good parent, they too might have gone shopping.

A relatively common issue is if your child prefers the lack of rules at their OP's house. The OP does not require them to finish their homework, for example. Or they are allowed to stay up late playing video games. In this situation, a clear contrast between homes might not endear your child to you. If you are too firm at enforcing your rules, your child, like others, may prefer the easier "more fun" parent. In those situations, you will need to compromise. Ask your child about their short-term goals, such as completing the school year. Talk about process. How can your child achieve those goals? For example, can your child accomplish some homework at their OP's house and what would make your home more fun? Do not be afraid to negotiate but do make a few changes that your child suggests. The most important thing is to *listen*. If your child feels that you *hear* them, you will retain your ability to influence them. Things might not happen on your timeline, but better to be able to participate in your child's life and influence their choices, than to be cast aside as the evil oppressor that the OP claims you to be.

HELPING YOUR CHILD NAVIGATE LIFE IN TWO HOMES

Your child is living in two homes that are vastly different from each other. This can be very confusing. But even young children can understand that customs and rules are different in mom's and dad's house. Any child who has been to pre-school or participated in activities such as Tee Ball has experienced different adults with assorted styles and rules. If your young child complains about something that happened at their OP's house, the simplest explanation is that their mother and father parent differently.

By middle school, your child is starting to develop executive functioning, which means that they can understand that things are not all black and white. They can articulate that their friends are not all the same and that each friend, like each relative, has good and bad traits. Each person has strengths and weaknesses. Ali may be good at math but bad at sports. Aiden might be great at soccer but hates to read. You should help them develop this understanding. Not only does it cultivate critical thinking skills, but it helps your child begin navigating their relationship with their OP. If the OP says or does something that disturbs or confuses them, you can point out how the people in their lives are different. Consider pointing out the differences between you and a grandparent or between two aunts. Point out that their OP may be good at their job and terrible at directions. Simply help them articulate their OP's different skills and personality traits. Help them identify their own unique personality traits. In this way, you are validating your elementary and middle school child's observations and feelings, while teaching them that they too have strengths and weaknesses, and that is normal and okay. This lesson will help them if they become too defensive of their OP. You can remind them that their OP, like everyone else, is not 100% good or 100% bad, and that they do not have to like everything about a person to maintain a relationship.

It is okay that your home environment is different from the OP's home environment. It may even be beneficial to emphasize those differences. I had a client who planned to pick up his son at 10:30 on Saturday morning. He then planned to drive his son to a pre-arranged playdate. The mother, however, had arranged for the son to sleep at a cousin's house on Friday night. She directed the son to call his father and ask to be picked up at 11:00 am. When the father asked why, the son had no answer. Nor could he explain his mother's refusal to allow the father to retrieve the son from the cousin's house, which was closer. Later, as they returned to the father's house, my client explained to his son that the mother's and son's choice to show up late to a pre-arranged playdate was rude if there was no *reason* to be late. By verbalizing the distinction between being late for a reason (dad's values) and being late for no discernable cause (mom's values), the father taught his son that there are diverse ways of doing things and in the father's house, courtesy is important. As this boy matures, he will be aware that timeliness is an issue that he should consider when making plans.

At some point, your child may sense that things are not "normal" in their OP's house. Perhaps there is too much fighting or too much neglect. Do not pretend that everything is normal in their OP's house if it is not. If your child expresses their truth, you must accept it as their truth, their experience. Otherwise, you will lose their trust. Validate your child's experiences and help them problem-solve.

In these situations, think of yourself as your child's coach. A baseball coach might point out that the third baseman on the other team has difficulty catching balls, so when your child is up to bat, they should aim for third base. Similarly, if your child is uncomfortable at their other parent's house help them find ways of coping. Brainstorming with them. For example, if your child's OP and the OP's new partner fight often, ask your child what they can do to avoid listening. Depending on their age, your child might need prompting, but potential solutions include going to their bedroom and turning on music, sitting outside for a while, or saving up for noise blocking earphones. Such solutions are workarounds. They do not focus on dialogue with the OP.

OPs are not receptive to complaints about their behavior, even from their child. Remember, they interpret criticism as demonization of their entire being. Thus, if you ask your child if they approached the OP with their problem, they may have said they tried and were unsuccessful, or that they did not. You should ask "why" to either answer. If your child tells you that they tried but failed because the OP got mad, or because they never finished the conversation (the OP is good at deflection), ask if they would be willing to try again. If so, help them find the right words. You may be concerned that you are setting your child up for failure because you know their OP is unresponsive to criticism, but this is their reality. As soon as they learn and accept their reality, they can begin looking for workarounds to solve their problems. You are also teaching your child how to have difficult conversations.

If your child says they did not try talking to their OP because they know by now that it is useless, it is appropriate to ask them how they feel. This is an important question. Not only are you encouraging your child's emotional intelligence, but you are also helping them understand that they are not responsible for the OP's reaction. Your follow-up question can be, "what do you think about your parent's reaction to your request?"

These types of conversations help your child begin realizing that they have choices when interacting with their OP. Knowing this, they will feel more empowered. You are also teaching them that some adults will listen to them, and some will not. If their OP is an adult that will not listen to them, then your child has learned another truth about that parent. And you did not disparage their OP. Instead, you helped your child begin learning how to navigate their increasingly complex life.

COUNTERING THE EFFECTS OF TOXIC PARENTING

Not all OPs are terrible parents. In fact, when their child is born, they often see the child as their clone. Many parents will say that their child is "just like them." They will love their baby as a reflection of themselves. Additionally, because the baby is dependent on them and they have control over providing for its needs, many OPs enjoy parenting their young children. That is not to say their love is disingenuous. Only that their relationship with their newborn may be tainted by how that baby reflects on them rather than seeing the baby as a separate person.

Problems may arise when the child grows and becomes more independent. During late elementary and middle school, it is age appropriate for a child to begin noticing the world beyond their immediate family and start making comparisons and contrasts. In high school, peer identity becomes especially important as children begin establishing their own identity. Along with puberty also comes the development of a person's Executive Functioning, which allows them to understand increasingly complex concepts. Many parents interpret this natural and appropriate progression as rejection and respond with anger. The relationship often improves when a child transitions from teenager to young adult. But the OP may be less tolerant and angrier than the average parent because they view the age-appropriate behaviors through a lens that interprets momentary rejection as a global rejection of their entire person, which is intolerable.

Being chronically combative is not a one-size-fits-all suit. Some are less volatile than others. Some are better at problem solving. Some do demonstrate empathy. The behaviors I see most often, however, are those I have mentioned previously:

- Limiting your child's participation in activities.
- Holding your children's possessions hostage.
- Disrespecting your children's privacy.

But the more egregious "parenting" is when the OP triangulates your child from you by forming a coalition against you. Because OPs have frail egos, they struggle with **Boundary Diffusion**.

Boundary Diffusion occurs when the relationship between the OP and their child is enmeshed. The parent believes that the child thinks and feels exactly as they do, and the child comes to accept this as true. When a young parent is preparing a toddler to go outside, if the parent is cold then they assume the child will be cold and dress the child accordingly. By school age, the child can tell the parent if they are hot or cold and there is recognition that the parent and child are separate individuals. When there is Boundary Diffusion, that separation fails to occur. The OP fails to acknowledge that the child is a separate individual and continues thinking that they are alike in every behavior, thought, and feeling. Feeling special, the child aligns with the OP and becomes a willing participant in the disruption of their natural development. Common characteristics of Boundary Diffusion are:

- The relationship between a child and the parent are enmeshed.
- The OP has difficulty distinguishing their own feelings from the child's.
- There is a fusion of thinking in which the child and their OP think alike.

These behaviors can corrupt a child's natural development. A child might sacrifice age-appropriate independent activities, such as going to summer camp, to stay close to their OP.

Boundary Diffusion manifests itself in two ways: as either **Parentification** or as **Infantilization**.

Parentification reverses the roles between parent and child. The adult enlists the child to perform adult tasks and to satisfy their own emotional needs. This parent:

- Treats the child like a peer or partner, sharing confidences.
- Enlists the child to fulfill their need for affection and care.
- Calls upon the child to comfort the parent about adult issues.
- Turns to the child for validation.
- Turns to the child for practical assistance even though such assistance is available through other sources.

Examples include having the older child, sometimes as young as eight, get themself and their younger siblings ready for school so that they can sleep in. Or depending on that child to be responsible for filling out school forms and advising the parent when it is time to drive to an activity.

These parents justify their choices by asserting, with pride, that their child "can manage it," and that their child is their "right hand." They exploit their child's eagerness, mistaking normal needs for acceptance and/or fear of rejection as "super-mature insight." This makes the child feel special and important.

Alternatively, a parent may be unable to tolerate a child's age-appropriate growth toward healthy independence. This is **Infantilization** and occurs when a parent keeps their child emotionally young. This parent limits the child's experiences and socialization to sustain the earlier dynamic of parent-dependent child. An example would be a parent who suggests their child should not participate in an activity because it is too hard, and they are fragile. One of my client's OP only permitted her child to play with children that were younger than her. She dressed her child in clothing she had outgrown. My client tried countering this by arranging playdates for his daughter with her classmates on his parenting time. This was successful at his house, but the girl struggled to make changes at her mother's house and continued playing with much younger children.

The effects of Parentification and Infantilization can be countered. Taking the direct approach with your child may be counterproductive. Children who become parentified feel protective of their OP. Children who are infantilized become dependent on their OP. In both scenarios, the child is subordinating their feelings for those of their parent. In one situation, an upper elementary school boy would return from his father's house depressed. This father knew that the mother suffered from depression. When living with her, this boy absorbed her feelings as his own. My client taught his son to differentiate his own feelings from his mother's, but it was difficult because the boy felt he was being loyal to his mother by sharing her feelings.

Children are not born understanding their own emotions. Newborns communicate their emotions and needs through their cries, and parents and caregivers learn to interpret them. Parents learn which cry means their child is hungry, tired, or that their diaper needs changing. Infants, in turn, learn about themselves. Without language, they learn that this feeling which created this cry means they are hungry because their parent brought them food and the feeling stopped. They learn that another feeling causes another type of cry, and their parent changed their diaper, so that feeling must have meant they were uncomfortable. But again, the infant has no language for these emotions.

As babies grow into toddles, their range of emotions expands. They may feel happy or sad, but they still lack the language to describe those feelings. It is up to the parent to teach their child to understand their feelings, by teaching them the vocabulary of language. Parents often do this by saying things such as "you look happy" or "did you have fun?" In this way, a child learns to label their feelings.

Try to remain cognizant of your own feelings. Many of us were taught not to express negative emotions. "Don't be angry," was a common admonishment. We now know that feelings are like water behind a dam. They will build and eventually bust through. If you were taught to suppress your feelings, do not. When you feel angry or sad, acknowledge that to your child. Explain how all feelings are acceptable but all behaviors are not.

Help your child identify and accept all their feelings, even the so-called negative feelings. From an early age, ask your child if they feel angry or anxious and help them find the words to describe their feelings. Questions such as "were you thinking and feeling that what happened was unfair?" or "were you thinking and feeling that what you had to do was scary?" Then affirm with labels such as "it sounds like you were angry" or "it sounds like you were anxious." Just like an infant learns to associate feelings with physical needs, young children need to learn to associate feelings with words.

As the children grow older, their feelings become more complex. Exposed to a world that does not include their parents, such as school, extracurricular activities, and part time jobs, they begin experiencing a broader range of emotions that can include stress, anxiety, and fear.

When they reach puberty, their ability to think abstractly develops. Now your child has new and complex thoughts but lacks the maturity to understand them. If their OP creates a home environment where they remain young, they may like that. Childhood is familiar and comfortable, and the world is a scary place. Alternatively, if the OP gives your child more responsibilities, telling them that they are really mature and can manage it, your child might like that because their OP trusts and relies on them. Either way, lacking an ability to process the complex world they live in, they adopt the thoughts and attitudes of their OP.

If you fear that your child is internalizing the thoughts and feeling of their OP, you must walk a delicate line in helping them identify and understand their own, independent feelings. Talking to them about the subject directly may cause them to become defensive. They may accuse you of disrespecting or not trusting them. You cannot say, for example, "that is not you speaking, that is your other parent." They will get angry. But if you foster your child's emotional intelligence without referencing their OP, you expose them to their own feelings and attitudes, which may be different from the OP's.

One of my client's children, who was in middle school at the time, proudly informed her mother that she had helped her father resolve a problem with someone at work. This child was looking for the same praise she received from her father. Failing to receive it, she was disappointed in her mother. Telling her that she is too young to be solving daddy's problems would anger her. The better approach would be to identify her feelings and apply them to other situations. The mother could ask, "how does it feel to help people?" Suppose this girl had previously helped her sibling or a friend. The mother might reference those other times, pointing out that her interest in helping people is not limited to helping her father. The mother might say, "you are good at helping people and like doing it. Maybe, you will become a therapist one day." In this way, the mother would have broken the child's myopic connection between her desire to help and her OP.

If you learn that the OP has tasked your middle school child with waking their younger siblings and getting them ready for school while the OP sleeps, you will not accomplish anything by telling your child that they are doing their OP's job. First, neither you nor your child have any power in the OP's home. Second, your child probably has mixed feelings about their situation. On one hand they may be resentful, but on the other, they may be proud of being tasked with these enhanced responsibilities. But they are too young to understand the complexities of their emotions. Suggesting they are wrong for doing what their OP asks of them, will make them defensive and angry.

Instead, ask them questions about how they would manage different situations. What would they do if they had gone to bed late the night before, and wanted to sleep in? Would they sacrifice their nighttime activity to get up early the next morning? By asking these questions, you are accomplishing two goals. First, you are helping your child problem-solve for unanticipated situations. Second, you are subtly suggesting that they should not always subordinate themselves for their OP.

In both situations, you are focusing on your child's needs and feelings and tacitly teaching that they can be different from their OP's.

If your child starts becoming fearful and you are concerned about infantilization, have them do increasingly more challenging activities. Take them roller blading or hiking. Do the activity with them. If you fall, demonstrate how you laugh and continue. If your child is tired, take a break with them and then suggest that you both try to go a little further. Use encouraging statements such as "I think you can do it." No matter how little they succeed, praise them for each step forward. The goal is to build their confidence. When they succeed, ask the how they feel? Highlight the satisfaction of achieving a goal.

You can also have this child help you cook or fold laundry. Maybe they will discover that they like vacuuming. Again, each task that you do together should give the child comfort because you are with them, and a growing sense of independence. Do not offer commentary about how their OP prevents them from participating in age-appropriate activities. The more your child gets out in your community, the more likely they are to come to that conclusion themself.

Help your child enhance their emotional intelligence by Role Modeling your own self-awareness. You will not always be in control of your emotions. No one is. But if an argument between you and your child becomes too loud and volatile, acknowledge that you are feeling overwhelmed. Ask your child if they feel that way too. Then talk about what the two of you can do. Perhaps you both need a "time out." Perhaps some self-care is in order. By openly discussing the process of identifying feelings and appropriate responses, you are teaching your child emotional intelligence, problem-solving skills, and personal boundaries.

TEACHING BOUNDARIES, CRITICAL THINKING, AND PROBLEM-SOLVING, SKILLS

As soon as you receive a Judgment of Divorce or Parenting Plan, your child is legally obligated to spend time with their OP. They now experience an entire world without you there to protect them. It is difficult to get the Family Court System to intervene. They are primarily concerned with ensuring a parent's legal rights. If your child is healthy, clothed, fed, and going to school, there is little you can do to get the court to stop the OP from making parenting choices that you see as harmful.

This is especially true when you are standing before a judge and the OP delivers a sincere and reasonable explanation for their behavior. It is painful to stand back and watch your child get hurt. Harder still knowing that the OP's actions are motivated by a desire to hurt you. You cannot talk to the OP, and you cannot rely on the court. But what you *can* do is teach your child the skills they need to manage their relationship with their OP. These skills include:

- Learning to set boundaries.
- Learning to think critically.
- Learning to problem solve.

TEACHING BOUNDARIES

When you walk away from someone who is yelling at you, you are demonstrating healthy safety boundaries. When you take a "parent time out" to recuperate and take care of yourself, you are demonstrating healthy emotional boundaries. As your child's role model, they will observe and learn from you. You can also teach them how to enforce their own boundaries.

If your child feels socially insecure or bullied at school, martial arts classes will teach them self-defense skills which will build their confidence. There are many books on how to help your child build confidence. But when the bully in their life is their OP, and they are legally bound to live with that parent, you and your child may feel helpless. It is difficult for a young child to physically escape a parent. And you cannot drive over to the OP's house and rescue them. What you can do, however, is honor their feelings and support their efforts to set *their* boundaries.

I know a young man who, at twelve years old, locked himself in the bathroom at his father's house to escape his father's wrath. He called his mother and they talked for 4 hours until he was ready to leave the bathroom. Another boy left his mother's house at night and began walking to his father's house. On the way he called his father, who picked him up and returned him to his mother's house. The father explained to his teenage son that the judge would punish him if he kept his son at his own house. This happened twice. The second time, when he returned to his mother's house, his aunt and uncle were there, and they helped him negotiate the conflict with his mother.

In both instances, the parents honored their child's feelings of being unsafe and unhappy. In both instances, the parents supported their child's effort to create boundaries. Neither parent violated their court orders and both parents guaranteed their child's safety. The mother by remaining on the phone. The father by picking his son up and returning him to his mother's house. In both instances, the children learned that it was okay for them to feel scared and angry and that their parent would support them within the limits of their ability. As these young men mature and experience different challenges to their physical and emotional well-being, they will recognize and honor their feelings and be better able to craft boundaries appropriate to the situation.

TEACHING CRITICAL THINKING, AND PROBLEM-SOLVING, SKILLS

Teaching your child to develop Critical Thinking, and Problem-Solving Skills will help them understand their situation from a more rational and less emotional perspective. The Oxford Dictionary defines Critical Thinking as "the objective analysis and evaluation of an issue in order to form a judgment." It is a process in which a situation is not accepted at face value but is examined and evaluated against known facts.

When your child tells you about something that happened at their OP's house that sets off your inner alarm, you must suppress your instinct to protect them and remind yourself that your job is to teach them the skills they need to resolve the problem themself. Your first question to your child then, is simply, "do you want to talk about it?"

The answer is often "no." If your child appears upset, remind them that they must honor their feelings and that there is a solution to whatever problem they face. Those simple words should reduce any feelings of helplessness they have and get them to begin pondering solutions. Eventually, your child might seek your help in resolving their problem with their OP. When that happens, ask your child why they think their OP made the choices that caused your child's discomfort. Do not react with negative statements that will lead your child to anger. Do not say, for example, "that is awful." This may backfire on you. Your child wants you to support *them*, not feed them *your* perspective.

If your child says that they do not know why their OP did or said something, you *can* feed them possibilities. Were they angry? Were they stressed? Regardless of the answer, the next focus of the discussion is to ask what your child thinks they can do. Again, ask them if they could have talked with their OP. Could they have taken care of the problem themself? One of my client's OP kept the bathroom towels on a shelf that was too high for their daughter to reach, making it difficult for her to shower. No one in the house would help. Brainstorming solutions helped the child problem-solve. Was there a stepladder available? Could she bring her own towel to his house? Would she be willing to use a towel that another person had used? Even if you and your child cannot think of a satisfactory solution to the problem, the act of brainstorming teaches problem-solving skills.

When I teach legal classes, I have my students play what I call the **What If Game**. I present a short hypothetical scenario and ask them to apply the appropriate law. Once they have done that, I change one or two facts, then ask if they would reach the same conclusion. This process demonstrates that while situations may appear similar, closer inspection might reveal that they are not. How does that help your child learn critical thinking skills? Earlier I mentioned how two parents can define the word "respect" differently. One parent may believe respect requires absolute adherence to the adult's wishes. The other parent may believe respect requires each person in the family to accommodate each other's reasonable requests. A child who lives in two households, where both parents talk about respect but define it differently, may be confused. But understanding that things *are* different in each of their parent's home, will help them navigate living in both.

The boy who parroted his mother and told his father that he would not be available at the pre-arranged 10:30 am pickup was unable to explain why. But by asking "why" the father encouraged his son to try to think of an answer. That there was no reasonable answer is as powerful a lesson as if there was one. Asking "why" moves the conversation from reaction to analysis. For example, suppose you go online to make reservations at your favorite restaurant. It is 2022 and restaurants are packed as people enjoy getting out after the Covid-19 Pandemic restrictions. But when you make the reservation, the restaurant wants a $25 nonrefundable deposit, per person. This is outrageous! You have been going to this place for years and they have never asked you for a nonrefundable deposit. Critical thinking suggest you consider why the restaurant made this choice. It is probably because too many people were making reservations and then not showing up, and the restaurant was trying to financially recover from two years of low income.

That is an easy thing to figure out. Critical Thinking is harder when you must evaluate the words and behavior of people to whom you have a strong emotional connection. We are biologically wired to want parental love. There are many books and movies about adults who finally learn that their parent was abusive. Or that the love they received was unhealthy love. The hero in the tale struggles to accept their flawed parent and to accept and love themself as well. Even children of parents who were not abusive but not great parents, eventually come to terms with those character flaws. Teaching your child to critically think furthers that healthy process.

Critically thinking requires you to ask "why." Thinking about what motivated a person to say or do something, not only helps your child develop insight into human nature, but insight into themselves as well. When your child complains about someone, ask them why they think the person made that choice. One of my client's had a teen-age daughter who was upset because her father purchased a new computer for his stepdaughter and gave her the old, broken computer to use. If she did not understand that he was trying to impress his new wife, she might have internalized his choice as proof that he thinks she is not worthy of a new computer. Identifying other motivations will not lessen her resentment, but it will provide context for the OP's decision.

Another client had a young daughter whose elementary school was hosting a daddy-daughter dance. The girl was excited. Unfortunately, the father could not leave work early enough to collect his daughter from her mother's house and get her to the dance on time, so he asked the mother to bring the daughter to the school. She agreed. When he arrived, he could not locate his daughter. She was not at the dance. Eventually he found her huddled with her mother. When he suggested they go to the dance, she refused. She then insisted she go home with her mother and threw a temper tantrum until he eventually let her do what she wanted. Obviously, the father was extremely disappointed and felt betrayed by the mother. When he finally has the opportunity to speak to his daughter about what happened, she could not tell him why she had changed her mind about the dance. Asking her if her mother said anything to her would not be wise as the daughter might become defensive. Worse is if it is too difficult for the daughter to understand and articulate her feelings (which, at that age, it usually is) and therefore accepts her mother's perspective as her own. The better approach was to offer the daughter choices. Were you afraid? Were you tired? Were you lonely? Did you miss your mom? Whatever option the daughter selects, regardless of whether it was true or not, provides an opportunity for the father to teach her Critical Thinking Skills. If she was afraid, for example, they could talk about what made her fearful and what she could do to overcome her fears. Providing options teaches a child both problem-solving and critical thinking skills because the conversation moves from accepting emotionally motivated behavior carte blanche, to understanding behavior based on facts and circumstances.

Critical thinking also requires you to assess what you see or hear against what you know. One of my client's had a parenting plan where the children lived with each parent 50% of the time. At one point her middle-school daughter complained that she did not see her father enough. This young girl was becoming enmeshed with her OP and starting to accept his version of the world as her own. By pulling out the calendar and having the daughter count the days she saw each parent, the mother taught a small lesson in critical thinking: not to accept emotional complaints as truthful facts.

Your child may practice their critical thinking skills on you. They may challenge you by asking you why you did something or pointing out that you said something different yesterday. When that happens, applaud them for their efforts and answer honestly. It is important that they feel comfortable challenging you. Knowing that you will own your own mistakes, creates a significant contrast with their relationship with their OP. In your house, your child will learn people make mistakes, that people can correct their mistakes, and that if you accept your mistakes, you will certainly accept theirs.

To correct a mistake, one must problem solve. Do not ask your child to help you. That is not their job. But you can tell them what you have decided to do and report back to them how well you succeeded. If your child wants to help you and offers you their solution to your problem, thank them and say that you will consider their suggestion. But do not begin talking about it. Your child should not feel responsible for solving your problems.

On the other hand, it is a parent's job to help their child solve their problems. Problem solving can be fun. Brainstorming solutions to problems can generate silly ideas. When helping your child solve a problem, start by accepting everything that you and your child think of, no matter how outrageous. Laughing about a crazy solution makes the problem feel less oppressive. When you do not have any more ideas, rank the top five. Number one should be your child's ideal solution. One of the reasons to have more than one solution is to teach your child that the first effort may not solve the problem. One of my favorite sayings is, **Plan B is your best friend**. Or Plan C. If you have a list of additional options, you do not feel as discouraged should Option A fail.

Teaching your child emotional self-awareness, how to maintain personal boundaries, critical thinking, and problem solving, skills is like teaching math. First your child learns to count. Then they learn simple addition and subtraction. Then multiplication. And eventually they learn algebra. It is a process. And each lesson builds on the next. The lessons do not need to be formal. You might talk as you are carrying the groceries inside or driving to a friend's house. But *have* the conversations. Make them part of your family culture. Because these skills will help your child adjust to living in two distinct homes. It will give them the ability to assess and understand the complexities of their life. And it will help them as they venture out into the world.

Teaching your child to negotiate with others, including their OP, will empower them. They will learn to respond to their OP's emotional and cyclical thinking, their deflection, and all the other strategies they use for enforcing their reality, with logic.

NEGOTIATING WITH YOUR YOUNG AND PRE-TEEN CHILD

Children are not born knowing how to handle conflict. It is a skill you must teach them. Your first conflicts with your young child begin when they are about two years old. That is when they start asserting themselves, using the only word they know: "No!" These times can be trying for a parent but forcing them to accept your wishes is a power play that teaches them they are subordinate to you. They do not learn that problems and conflicts can be resolved.

At two-years-old, your child is in the infant stages of self-reflection. They feel troubled but do not know why. They lack the vocabulary or experience to express themselves. You can teach them by offering choices. Ask, for example, "do you want Cheerios or yogurt for breakfast?" This exposes your child to the fact that options are available. They begin learning that they have some autonomy, even if it is only to choose their breakfast.

It takes patience. Mornings are always hectic for working parents. Do your best to remain calm. If your stress levels elevate, so will your child's. Emotions are contagious. Even an infant can sense their parent's feelings. Your child will channel your anxiety and everyone's emotions will elevate. It is an unpleasant Catch-22. But offering your child choices at an early age teaches them that problems can be solve, that they have autonomy over their life, and that they can influence you.

This last lesson will become extremely important when your child become a teenager. If your teenager feels that you never listen to them and that you believe you are always right, they are more likely to rebel in ways that are harmful to themself.

No one wants to be in a relationship where they are always wrong, especially young adults who are just figuring out who they are and how they fit in the world. They will only let you influence them if they feel they can influence you too. They want to feel they have some autonomy in their lives. They want to feel that you respect them. I talk more about the teenage years later in this Chapter.

Teaching negotiation skills accompanies teaching emotional intelligence. I have seen frustrated parents in the parking lot of a store dragging their screaming child to the car. Sometimes the parent tries ignoring their child. Sometimes the parent shouts at their child. Neither stops the tantrum. And both are counterproductive because the child senses and absorbs their parent's stress. Whatever initially upset them (you did not buy them candy, or they are hungry, or tired) their tantrum intensifies. We have all been in these situations and understand how frustrating and stressful they can be.

But what if you stopped for a moment, held your child, and said, "I know you are upset and when we get to the car, we can talk about it." Even if that does not stop the crying, you have told your child that you are sympathetic to their pain. You are honoring their feelings. And they are learning that the name of this feeling is "upset."

It is, of course, difficult to set aside your own frustration and embarrassment to acknowledge your child's feelings. You may be angry at your child for putting you in this situation when you have things to do, and time is short. If so, try listening to your inner voice. Are you thinking, "why should I take this?" or "I am the parent here?" Unfortunately, these thoughts increase your anger. Changing the dialogue inside your head will change your perspective. If you said to yourself, for example, "I see my child is so upset and can't manage their feelings right now," you are better able to calm yourself and your child.

Solving your child's problem for them misses an opportunity to teach them problem solving skills. If your toddler refuses to put on their winter coat, for example, forcing them will again suggest that their wishes are not being honored. I am not suggesting that you allow your child to go out in subzero temperatures without a coat. But a power-play will make the situation worse. Toddlers tend to dig in their heels, and they will feel they are being punished even if you are trying to protect them from the cold.

Your first step is to tell them they will be cold. But that is an abstract concept that a toddler may not understand. Opening the door might help. If not, or if you are pressed for time, saying, "okay, but if you are cold, I have your coat," tells your child that:

1. You heard them,
2. They do not need to be stubborn to assert themselves,
3. You have their back,
4. Mistakes can be fixed, and
5. Chilly weather requires a coat.

It is not "giving in" to give them what they want, within reason. If your child's request is reasonable, try not to reject it simply because you had another plan. If their request is unreasonable, explain why. Children also need to learn that they will not get everything they want and that there are times when gratification must be delayed.

Sometimes, your child's problem is with you. When your child has a conflict with you, do your best to remain detached and not defensive. In the Netflix series *Sweet Magnolias*, a character's teenage daughter wanted to help her mother eat better by removing sugary foods from the cupboard. The mother snapped at her, saying that she could take care of herself. As the daughter stormed out of the kitchen, she accused her mother of always having to be right. That scene stuck with me because the mother, a single parent, was alienating her daughter by pushing her out. She did not consider how her daughter was experiencing their relationship. The mother was ignoring the person who comprised 50% of that relationship.

In relationships, when the issue *is* the relationship, being "right" is often a matter of perspective. The mother in that scene felt she was right by not permitting her daughter to care for her. She felt that was the mother's job. The daughter felt it was not right for her mother to isolate herself. Who is actually "right?" The answer is neither. The two people in the relationship must manage it in a way that is rewarding for both. No one can always be "right" in a relationship. The other person will eventually walk away. If your child's issue is with you then, do your best to listen. Some part of what they have to say, may be "right."

NEGOTIATING WITH YOUR TEENAGER

Many parents believe that teenagers need firm boundaries because they are so susceptible to outside influences. The problem with that approach, when your child has an OP who competes with you for their love, is that the OP may take advantage of your attitude by becoming increasingly liberal, to entice your child to live with them. A teenager's exposure to outside influences causes them to question everything, including their family. This is age-appropriate development. A parent must find the sweet spot between respecting their teenager's growth and continuing to prepare them for life as productive adults and teaching them cultural values.

A teenager needs to know that you support *their* journey and that you are helping them prepare for their adult life. This starts with discussing or negotiating with your teenager. Suppose you allow your 16-year-old to borrow your car to go to a friend's home. You ask your teenager what time they think they will be home. They say 11:00. It is a school night, so you say 10:00. They tell you that they finished their homework. You and your teenager compromise and they agree to be home at 10:30.

Now suppose 10:30 has come and gone and your teenager is not home. You call their cell phone, but they do not answer. At 11:00 your teenager walks into the house. They tell you that they and their friend met some people at a restaurant, and it took a while to pay the bill. They also tell you that their phone had no battery left.

Your teenager has defied you and breached your agreement. If you ignore this, they may do it again. If you punish them; they will be angry at you. They will argue that you are being unfair because coming home late was not their fault. While that is true, your teenager had told you they would be at their friend's house, not at a restaurant.

Your teenager wants autonomy. You want to know where they are and for them to be safe. Perhaps you were tired and wanted to go to sleep, but you had to stay awake until your teenager returned home. *Now* the real negotiation with your teenager begins.

Your teenager will have an abundance of reasons why they defied you and the agreement. It is important to listen with an open mind. Your teenager made a choice without considering the possible outcomes. Asking why they left without charging their phone and why they did not call to let you know they were going to a restaurant, focuses on their choices and what different choices they might have made instead.

But the conversation should not stop there. A relationship involves more than one person. Your teenager should understand how their choice affected you. Telling them how tired you are, but that you could not sleep until they came home, will emphasize the negative consequence of their choice. At the time, they probably thought that being a half an hour late was not a big deal. They were thinking of themself and not you. What is the outcome of this conversation? Your teenager must keep their cell phone charged and must call you if their plans change.

By listening to your child's explanation with an open mind, your child will listen to you. They become willing to include you as one factor of their decision making.

Another example is if your adult daughter plans to go hiking with a friend. When you ask for her to allow you to track her cell phone, she accuses you of invading her privacy. If you demand that she gives you access or you will not allow her to go, she will be even angrier. She is not thinking of the consequences of her decision. You can help her by explaining them. Do not be dramatic. Do not talk about all the bad things that might happen to two young women in the woods. That would either discourage her from becoming more independent, or she will think you are being ridiculous. Instead, try to make your explanation lighthearted. In a similar situation, I once told my child, "I promise not to stalk you, but if something happens to you, I don't want to be the parent who tells the police officer that I have no idea where you are." My child laughed and agreed to let me track their phone.

In both scenarios, you would be supporting your child's choice of activity while holding a tether in case they have a problem. You are there for them if they need you, but only if they agree to keep the metaphorical door open. One reason your child might agree to this is that it is no different than how you have been parenting them since they were born. You have always provided them space to grow and explore and you have always been there when they needed you.

Consider this: when your child was an infant, the world you provided for them consisted of their crib and a play pen. When they started crawling, their world expanded to an entire room, probably with a gate on it. When your child began school, their world grew to your home, the school, and perhaps some friends' houses. During all this time, you were there supporting and protecting them. Now that your child is a teenager, their world expands to the boundaries of your community. Sometimes beyond if they travel with their class or youth group. Your teen wants and needs the freedom to explore. Exploration helps them learn about themself and is part of their natural development. They need guidance, which is why it is important to talk about the decisions they made. There are times when they will need to be responsible for the consequences of those decisions. But if you ask them to let you help should they find themselves in a difficult situation, they are likely to agree and give you access to their cell phone.

It is easy to become exasperated when a teenager challenges your every norm and value. When your teen defies you, it is hard to remember that their struggle to become an individual who is independent from their family is part of their natural development. Remember that their motives are not about you. I had a client whose teenage son was preparing for his high-school graduation. When he emerged from his room, he was wearing shorts and a tee shirt. The mother told him to dress appropriately. The teen said that no one would see what he wore under his robe. Exasperated, the mother drove the son to the shopping mall and bought him a suit to wear, griping about why he was doing this to her. The mother did not understand that her teen's decision had nothing to do with her. Perhaps his friends were wearing shorts and tees under their robes, and he wanted to dress like them. Perhaps he thought he would be hot in a suit. Whatever his reasons, it is unlikely the boy's original thought was to wear shorts just to irritate his mother. But because she took his behavior personally, it became about rebelling against her, and their day of celebration was diminished.

Be sympathetic regardless of how irrational your teen sounds. Let them know that it is their problem to overcome, but that you will be there to help. Your teen will hear you better if you express compassion. When your teenager says or does something that sets off alarm bells, try not to immediately begin by pointing out the flaws in their thinking. Be mindful of how you question them. If you begin by interrogating your teen, or your teen feels you are not listening, they will shut down. Instead, try to be curious and respectful. Ask questions first and make sure they are open ended. Do not, for example, say, "Did you *really* think that was a good idea?" This question invites a yes or no answer, which will not move the conversation forward. Try instead, "Why did you decide to do that?" Now you are asking your teen in a non-judgmental way (check your tone of voice!) to explain themself. Then listen to their answer. Hear their point of view. Ask follow-up questions. Perhaps their thought process started off logically and only became misguided at the end. In that case, talk about what your teen might have done differently. Help them think through the problem with the benefit of hindsight. And hopefully, with the benefit of your wisdom as well.

A common negotiating tactic in business is to find the "win-win." That is a solution where both parties gain something they want while giving up something else. Neither party walks away feeling that they lost everything, and the other party was the absolute winner. By compromising, your teen will feel they were able to influence you. In turn, they will be more wiling to accept your influence.

Sometimes it may be useful to assist in their rebellion. If a cis male child begins wearing women's clothing and makeup, he is either experimenting or rebelling, or both. You can rail against him. You can argue that he is not being genuine to himself or that he will not be received well when he goes out into the world. But doing so may cause a stubborn child to dig in their heels to prove that they are now transgender. Another option is to "go with the flow" instead of "spiting into the wind." Help your son buy clothes and makeup and negotiate guidelines about when the cis son can wear them. If he really is just experimenting, the experiment will be shorter than if the behavior is motivated by the need to prove himself "right" to his parents. Remember that everything changes, and this phase will pass.

Because your teen's world is complicated and much of it no longer includes you, and because your teen is still learning how to make sense of their world, and because they are teenagers with fluctuating hormones, your child's emotions may swing from highs to lows. It is important to tolerate your child's pain without trying to fix the problem for them. You must help them fix it by offering support and guidance, but you cannot rush in and save them no matter how much you want to. Standing beside your child while they suffer their pain and anger and being with them while they try to fix their problem and fail, teaches them to tolerate themself when they are miserable and unsuccessful. If you support and love them through their struggles, they will learn to love and support themself.

Never deny your child their feelings. Do not say "you are not angry," or "don't feel that way." Your teenager lives in a complicated world, made more difficult by living in two distinct homes. Technology, fads, political, and social events change every day. Teenagers are bombarded with issues and challenges to their self-esteem, especially on social media. They live in a world that does not always contain you. When they are with their OP, they are in a world that you can never enter. You may never know what all their struggles are. They are trying to make sense of *their* world. They are trying to find their place and understand who they are. Parents do not know everything their teen experiences and encounters. They only know what the teen tells them. If you are compassionate and ask them what they want and how you can help, if the two of you work together, your teen will understand that you will always have their back. Supporting their journey, rather than dictating its course, will cement your relationship now and in the future.

COMMON PARALLEL PARENTING PITFALLS

Remember that your child is a victim. They did not choose their family structure and yet they are required to navigate it, sometimes from an early age. Do not impose a "price" for having a relationship with you. Your relationship with your child should never be "either-or." Your child has a right to love both parents, regardless of how evil you perceive their other parent to be.

Try not to dismiss your child's feelings by claiming they are parroting their other parent. Your child is entitled to own their feelings, even if the words were provided to them. Additionally, you child is continuing to experience life outside your domain. Those experiences change them, and they are no longer the same person they once were. Nor should you accuse them of being ignorant and not "not knowing what they are talking about." That may be true, but they are probably experimenting with new ideas and words and are looking to you for guidance, not to be shut down. Children, especially teenagers, try on new ideas like clothing. Instead of challenging them, ask them why they said what they did and help them critically think.

Be mindful of criticizing your child too frequently. No one responds well to that. Instead, try to "catch them being good," so that they feel good about themselves. Emotions are contagious. If you are too negative towards your child, they are likely to become more negative towards you. This will increase everyone's stress. Catching them being good breaks that cycle and reduces the negative impact when you do need to correct their behavior.

Do not be passive, thinking that if you give them space they will "come to their senses." Doing so risks the possibility that your child perceives your withdrawal as lack of love and concern. Do not give up parenting time. If your teenager has a social engagement on your time, have them leave from your house and return there. Even if you think you are doing them a favor by letting them stay the weekend at their other parent's house and go to the party from there, your teen might misinterpret your inaction as failing to care.

One problem many single parents face is the support they receive from loving friends and family. The people in your life support you. They will reinforce that your child's other parent is a bad person. They may point out their flaws. While the support is comforting, the words are not helpful. Constantly hearing how awful the OP is, makes it much more difficult for you to Mindfully Disengage and Mindfully Engage. Hearing that the other parent "should" do something creates unrealistic expectations, no matter how much you agree. To successfully disengage from your child's other parent and reduce the stress in your life, you must manage the real person, as they are, and not as you wish them to be. Also, if your child overhears, they may resent your family for disparaging their other parent. There is a risk of a rift forming between your child and your extended family.

Finally, do not allow your sadness, anger, or stress cloud the environment in your home. If your home is depressing, your child will resist being there. Making your home a place where they want to be, encourages them to return.

CREATING A CHILD CENTERED HOME

Every person wants their home to be a place where they are fully accepted. A place where their bad moods, anger, and anxiety are tolerated. Where their poor choices will be forgiven. Everyone wants their home to be a safe harbor.

Creating a home that is a safe place for you and your child can be accomplished by mindfully developing a family culture. Family culture is also a strong counterweight to the toxicity generated by the OP, or your child's school, or work environment. A family culture that is welcoming and tolerant makes a space where you and your child will *want* to be.

I learned the power of family culture when my son was young. I had arranged a playdate at the house of a girl he knew from preschool. At the end of the playdate, the little girl returned all the toys to the toy-cabinet without being asked by her mother. In my house, we cleaned up the toys together. I asked the mother how she had taught her daughter to clean up on her own. The mother looked at me and said, "that's just the way we do it."

This mother had created a culture that included putting away toys after using them. It is a small example, but powerful. If a child grows up in a house where everyone complains, the family has a culture of dissatisfaction. It will be what the child knows and displays. I know a boy whose father gained full custody when he was in high school. When he lived with his mother, grades were not important to him. They lived in a neighborhood where his peers were comfortable with mediocre grades, and she did not focus on his education. When he moved into his father's house, the culture was vastly different. He was not told to work harder. Nor was he punished for bad grades. But his siblings and step siblings were invested in their education and were strong students. They spent time working on their homework. His father and stepmother worked hard at their jobs too. Eventually, this young man adopted the culture of hard work, and it became important to him. Now he has a successful professional job of which he is proud. Family culture matters.

There are many other ways to make your home a haven for your child. They include:

- Sharing your child's interests.
- Strengthening inter-family relationships.
- Making work a group activity.
- Making time to play.
- Creating traditions and rituals.

SHARING YOUR CHILD'S INTERESTS

When I was growing up my parents told me to turn off my music. They argued that it had not withstood the test of time. Many years later, I tried introducing my parents to that very same music. They were still not interested. What my parents failed to realize was that by refusing to spend even a few minutes listening, they denied us something that we might have shared. You do not need to like the same things your child enjoys but making the effort will not only make them feel valued, they will be more open to experiencing the things that *you* value.

Additionally, do your best to attend all your child's activities even if they fall on the OP's parenting time and the drive is inconvenient. If you have joint legal custody, you have the right to be there. Not only does your presence show support for your child, but it demonstrates to the OP that they failed in thwarting you. Be mindful of the OP's reaction, however. They sometimes complain that you are monopolizing your child's time on *their* parenting time. If that happens, try not to approach your child. Wait for your child to come to you and do not spend too long talking. Arrange to talk to them later. The concern is that the OP will file a motion asking the judge to prevent you from attending your child's events on their time. Rather than risk this, it is better to back off for a while until the OP moves on to another issue to complain about. Finally, consider participating in your child's activities by coaching, fundraising, or coordinating the end of the year party. Doing so not only demonstrates your support for your child, but it may also give you a little extra time with them that you would not otherwise have.

It is important that your children have good relationships with each other. There is no one who experiences what life is like in your house *and* in the OP's house other than your children and their siblings. Cultivating the sibling relationship will help them process their childhood as they grow older. Knowing there is someone in their life who shared their childhood experiences is very comforting. And if your children can talk about those experiences, they might gain insights that will help them adjust to past traumas.

There are many ways to support sibling relationship. One is to have each child attend their sibling's activities to show their support. Another is to rotate which family member selects the family fun activity each week, and to make sure that everyone participates, even if they do not like the selection. Explain that when they support their sibling's choice, their sibling will support theirs. If your children start bickering when they play games together, remind them that the purpose is to have fun. If they do not like the rules of the game, they can change them so that everyone is happy.

Family meetings provides another opportunity to bond. They can be formal {with an agenda} or informal {an opportunity to "check-in}. They can be about weekly schedules but should include issues. Everyone should have an opportunity to discuss something that troubles them. The others should listen respectfully, even if the issue is about someone in the family. Teach your children how to air a grievance without personally attacking the other person. And teach your children how to listen to the person who feels hurt by them. By doing this, you are creating a family culture of acceptance and tolerance. You are creating a safe harbor.

MAKING WORK FUN

Everyone has work to do. Your child has homework. You have bills to pay, or you may have work that you brought home from your job. Instead of everyone doing their own work on their own agenda, try setting aside time where "everyone" does their work. Better still, take breaks together. After one hour of work, for example, pop popcorn in the microwave. Have everyone share what they are doing and what they are struggling with. Perhaps a sibling has an idea that can help. By demonstrating that you too have things to do, things that you do not necessarily enjoy, you are role modeling responsibility while creating bonds. Doing your work while your child is doing theirs is far better than nagging them to finish their homework.

You can also make chores fun. If everyone participates then no single chore should be too burdensome. One way is to have a "chore day." Write each chore on a piece of paper and have everyone select one or two from a hat. Another way is to have a short game of chore-bingo. Whoever wins gets to select their chore. Or simply play music and each week a different person gets to select the "chore tunes." After all the chores are finished, serve a favorite lunch that becomes a special "end of the chores" meal. If the snow needs to be shoveled, consider dividing the driveway into sections and having a contest for who can shovel the snow fastest. The winner gets the most marshmallows in their hot chocolate. There are many ways to make unenjoyable tasks more tolerable. Ask friends. Research ideas on Google. Watch a family friendly movie. Your family will not behave identically, but if chores can be done without anyone whining, then the day will be better for everyone.

MAKING TIME TO PLAY

Would you rather sit with a group of strangers who are laughing or who are crying? The answer is obvious. People like to play and have fun. And playing together creates bonds. We send our children on playdates, not on crying dates. We choose friends who make us laugh. While we will support our friends when they hit a rough patch, we would not choose them to be in our life if they were chronically unhappy.

Fun is important. If your children have fun with you, they will want to be with you.

Fun activities do not need to be expensive. Going on a cruise is fun, but so is flying a kite. Even grocery shopping can be fun if everyone gets silly or someone makes a joke.

Be available to play with your child. When they were young, you probably read to them and played games together. Do not stop.

They say laughter is the best medicine. I have written at length about expressing and honoring a family member's sadness and anger, but you do not want to live in The Crying House. Make time for your family to live in The Fun House.

CREATING TRADITIONS AND RITUALS

Traditions and rituals help families have fun together. They create bonds. And they give children something to look forward to. Growing up with family traditions, a child might say to their friend, "Our family does this on Halloween." The words "our family" reinforces the feeling that your child is part of something larger than themself. They are not alone. They are part of your family. Traditions and ritual contribute to a family identity.

It does not matter if the traditions and rituals are religious or secular, simple or elaborate. The important thing is that your family enjoys a particular activity at a specific time. Select or create activities that you think everyone will enjoy. But be open minded. You may need to try another if the first one falls flat. If you are struggling for ideas, do some online research. There are resources that will help. But be careful not to select something too cumbersome.

If the tradition is too difficult to implement, you might not want to do it again.

Traditions and rituals can be annual, weekly, or daily. Most families have daily routines that can be identified as rituals or traditions. The family eats dinner at 6:30 P.M., for example. But you can introduce something different and quirky. In the old television show *The Waltons*, the episodes always ended in the evening with the family members calling out good night to each other. Imitating that would be a small ritual that can feel both lighthearted and heartwarming. A weekly ritual might be Friday night game or movie night. An annual ritual might be a family snowball fight on the first day of the year that it snows.

Holidays offer an abundance of opportunities to create traditions and rituals. You probably already practice some. Do not succumb to feeling sad that your ex-spouse is no longer there to share the event. Looking back, you can probably remember several holidays that were less than pleasant because of your ex-spouse's temper. This is an opportunity to create new bonds with your children. One father began taking his children to synagogue every Saturday morning after he and his ex-wife divorced. This was not something they had done together when they were still married. But it was comforting for the father. He made friends. The children made friends. And everyone looked forward to the snacks that were served after the service. Another parent took his children camping every summer, something his ex-wife did not enjoy. And another took her child downtown every year to watch the lighting of the Hanukkah menorah and Christmas tree. These traditions and rituals will help you disengage from the OP. They will help your family grow closer. And give you, too, something to look forward to.

CONCLUSION

Life is change and this phase of your life will pass. The question is: what will the next phase look like? Will you be confident that you can achieve your goals? Or will you feel worn out and exhausted from the extended conflict you endured? Will your children be thriving, mentally and physically? Or will they be struggling with anxiety and depression?

There is a way forward to a happier life. Understanding yourself and the OP helps. Enforcing your boundaries is essential. And knowing what you want your family life to be and how to achieve it, gives you direction.

Your and your children's interactions with the OP should not impede you. By changing your responses, you teach the OP what is and is not acceptable. By teaching your children skills, they also learn what is and is not acceptable. You and the OP will still need to make some parenting decisions together, but now there will be structure and civility. You will no longer be at the far end of the co-parenting continuum. Now you will be somewhere in the middle along with most parents who do not get along but can occasionally make important parenting decisions together.

The path I have shown you is hard, but you do not need to be perfect. Accept that you will make mistakes. Acknowledge them to yourself and your child. And then move on to Plan B. Or Plan C.

Being a "good enough" parent is widely recognized as the benchmark for parenting. If your child knows deep in their heart that you have been and always will be there for them, they will forgive your mistakes and they will thrive.

WORKBOOK

STEPS TO HELP UNDERSTAND YOURSELF WHEN YOU INTERACT WITH THE OP

The goal of this exercise is to learn more about yourself when you are not at your best. We often hear that emotions such as anger, anxiety, or frustration are "negative." But these feelings are as much a part of you as your happiness and joy. Humans are complex creatures, and we change over time and with experience. The objective here is to understand who you are *now*. To embrace those feelings as you would embrace a friend who is struggling. And to learn how to manage those emotions so they are as empowering to you as feelings of love.

Set aside thirty minutes and find a dark, quiet space and a comfortable position to sit or lie down. List the five people in your life who you find most difficult to interact with.

1. ____
2. ____
3. ____
4. ____
5. ____

What characteristics do these people share that cause you discomfort?

1. ____
2. ____
3. ____
4. ____
5. ____

How does your body register your discomfort? For example, do you

- Get knots in your stomach.
- Clench your hands or jaw.
- Feel clammy or flushed.
- Breathe faster.
- Feel tension in your neck and shoulders.
- Suddenly need to pace.
- Or begin having difficulty concentrating?

1. ____
2. ____
3. ____
4. ____
5. ____

Sit with those feelings for a moment. Try not to quell them. It is important to understand how *you* register emotional pain or frustration. The next task is the most difficult: identifying *why* you feel uncomfortable. What about those characteristics trigger you? For example, I mentioned my college roommate who frequently lied. I found it extremely aggravating and moved out of that dorm room at the semester break. Years later I realized that what upset me was not the lie but her unwillingness to listen to me. To hear me. As a young child I often felt that I was not seen or heard, and my roommate's behavior triggered those childhood frustrations. Try equating your feelings with memories or events that caused you pain.

____
____
____
____

Consider taking a break now, to give yourself time to mull over what you have learned. Later, when you are ready, list the OP's characteristics or behavior that evoke the same response in you.

1. ____
2. ____
3. ____
4. ____
5. ____

Can you equate the OP's characteristics or behavior that evoke the same feelings and memories that you recorded above?

____
____
____
____
____

You have probably already thought about what attracted you to the OP initially, but can you identify what deeply rooted pains or injuries they touch and activate? Imago Theory postulates that we select partners our subconscious recognizes from the love we received in childhood. If that love was faulty, we select partners with similar faults. This knowledge is the "other side of the coin," if that coin represents your reason for selecting the OP. On one side of the coin are the OP's positive traits that attracted you. On the other side are the empty spaces inside yourself that some part of you thought they could fill. Knowing this about yourself will not only help you make better choices in the future but will help you understand *why* the OP engenders such rage or fear in you.

CHANGING HOW YOU RESPOND TO THE OP

The OP's narrative is that you are trying to take their child away from them. The narrative manifests itself in themes, such as:

- You are trying to interfere or reduce their parenting time.
- You do not respect them as a parent.
- You are trying to turn their child against them.
- You are trying to bankrupt them.
- You are controlling/demanding/mean/stubborn/unlikable, etc.

There may be more. Identify the themes the OP most frequently uses to attack.

1. ____
2. ____
3. ____
4. ____
5. ____

For each theme, list the topics the OP primarily relies on to support their narrative. For example, if the theme is interfering or reducing their parenting time, does the OP frequently ask you for schedule changes or deny your requests for schedule changes? If the theme is money, does the OP frequently refuse to pay for extra ordinary medical expenses or does the OP frequently demand money from you? And if the theme is your personality, what does the OP most often accuse you of. The goal is to identify **patterns** of behavior so the OP's actions and reactions can be more easily anticipated.

1. Theme _______________________________________
   Topic _______________________________________
   Topic _______________________________________
   Topic _______________________________________

2. Theme _______________________________________
   Topic _______________________________________
   Topic _______________________________________
   Topic _______________________________________

3. Theme _______________________________________
   Topic _______________________________________
   Topic _______________________________________
   Topic _______________________________________

4. Theme _______________________________________
   Topic _______________________________________
   Topic _______________________________________
   Topic _______________________________________

5. Theme _______________________________________
   Topic _______________________________________
   Topic _______________________________________
   Topic _______________________________________

Review your list and look for patterns of behavior. For example, when accusing you of not respecting them as a parent, does the OP claim that you disparage them in front of the children? How often do they make this accusation within three or six months? Do they always use email or are these accusations usually sent via text. Start with the most frequent topics raised by the OP within that three-to-six-month period.

1. Topic _______________________________________
   Pattern of Behavior: _______________________________

____

____

____

2. Topic ____
   Pattern of Behavior: _______________________________

   ____

   ____

   ____

3. Topic ____
   Pattern of Behavior: _______________________________

   ____

   ____

   ____

4. Topic ____
   Pattern of Behavior: _______________________________

   ____

   ____

   ____

5. Topic ____
   Pattern of Behavior: _______________________________

   ____

   ____

   ____

Once you are conscious of your behaviors in your interactions with the OP, you can decide if and how to change them. Do not judge yourself. Changing your behavior is difficult. Behavior can become habits. To make changes, you must first recognize what it is that you do. For example, do you

- Immediately tell the OP that they are wrong.
- Immediately insult them.
- Immediately tell them your opinion and why you are right.
- Shut down.

- Walk away.
- Scream or cry or feel the urge to hit something.

For each pattern of behavior the OP demonstrates, do your best to honestly describe your reaction.

1. OP Pattern ____
    Your Reaction: _______________________________________

2. OP Pattern ____
    Your Reaction: _______________________________________

3. OP Pattern ____
    Your Reaction: _______________________________________

4. OP Pattern ____
    Your Reaction: _______________________________________

5. OP Pattern ____
    Your Reaction: _______________________________________

Reflect on your list and decide what you would have preferred doing instead of what you did. This is the "what you would have done differently if you could go back and do it again" activity. When thinking about this, fantasy is not a bad place to start. Would you want, for example, to be like your favorite character in a book or television show? If so, what about that character appeals to you? For each reaction, consider how you would want to change.

1. Reaction: ____
    Preferred Reaction: __________________________________

2. Reaction: ____

   Preferred Reaction: ________________________________

3. Reaction: ____

   Preferred Reaction: ________________________________

4. Reaction: ____

   Preferred Reaction: ________________________________

5. Reaction: ____

   Preferred Reaction: ________________________________

Consider when and why you and the OP might have your next conflict. Can you visualize yourself behaving differently? Can you reasonably expect to have the perfect reaction? For example, Atticus Finch in *To Kill a Mockingbird*, was always a wise, measured, and brave character. I would like to be more measured in how I respond to situations too. Would I like to be as brave as Katniss Everdeen from *The Hunger Games*? Sure, but that will never happen. Be honest with yourself. If you are an impulsive person, for example, being more temperate might not be fully attainable, but you might teach yourself to be a little more moderate in your personal interactions. As you ponder, consider **how** you might change.

There are many ways to prompt change. You can, for example, keep a calendar or note on your cell phone and record each time you succeed. You can even give yourself a gold star. If this is your choice, consider also recording when you did not respond in the manner you wanted and reflect on the reasons. Do not expect to change your behavior immediately. It takes time and people have setbacks. But if you find that you are frequently unable to implement *this* change, maybe it is not right for you. Do not fear starting over with a new preference. Change is a **process**.

There are other ways to help you remember that you want to change your behavior. A quick search will help you find Apps that are designed for this purpose. Or you can put a sticker on your cell phone case with a picture or word that you identify with this change. Another option is to wear a rubber band or hair band on your wrist. Whenever you encounter the OP, snap it gently to remind yourself of your goal. People also keep small marbles or stones in their purse or pocket. Rubbing these also serves as a reminder of what you want to achieve.

For each preferred reaction, think about how you might start implementing the change.

1. Preferred Reaction: _______________________________________
   Step to Change: ____
   Step to Change: ____
   Step to Change: ____

2. Preferred Reaction: _______________________________________
   Step to Change: ____
   Step to Change: ____
   Step to Change: ____

3. Preferred Reaction: _______________________________________
   Step to Change: ____
   Step to Change: ____
   Step to Change: ____

4. Preferred Reaction: _______________________________
   Step to Change: _______________________________
   Step to Change: _______________________________
   Step to Change: _______________________________

5. Preferred Reaction: _______________________________
   Step to Change: _______________________________
   Step to Change: _______________________________
   Step to Change: _______________________________

It is important to give yourself a realistic measure of success. Consider whether changing your behavior 33% of the time is sufficient. Or would you prefer 60%? Do not impose a 100% success rate. That is too harsh. No one behaves exactly as they believe they should all the time. We get tired or stressed or distracted. There are a plethora of feelings and events that might interfere with our efforts. And you do not want to set yourself up to feel defeated.

1. Preferred Behavior: _______________________________
   Goal: _______________________________

2. Preferred Behavior: _______________________________
   Goal: _______________________________

3. Preferred Behavior: _______________________________
   Goal: _______________________________

4. Preferred Behavior: _______________________________________
   Goal: ____

5. Preferred Behavior: _______________________________________
   Goal: ____

Finally, do not forget to reward yourself. Give yourself something special when you achieve one-third of your goal, two-thirds of your goal, and 100% of your goal. Everyone needs positive reinforcement, and you deserve that gift too.

CREATING A PERSONAL PARENTING PLAN

If you are struggling to craft a Personal Parenting Plan, list the five most important characteristics you would want your child to have when they are thirty years old. Embedded within this list might be skills such as resourceful, organized, or able to laugh it off when things go wrong.

1. ____
2. ____
3. ____
4. ____
5. ____

Next, prioritize those traits.

1. Most Important: _______________________________________
2. Second Most Important: _________________________________

3. Third Most Important: ________________________
4. Fourth Most Important: ________________________
5. Fifth Most Important: ________________________

Consider how you would help them learn to acquire these selected traits. Things to think about may include what life lessons you want to teach them, what education they might need, what support could help them, such as tutors, coaches, or counselors, and what extracurricular activities would further these goals. For each of your five goals, prepare a list of three to five things you can do to achieve them.

1. Most Important:

a. ________________________
b. ________________________
c. ________________________
d. ________________________
e. ________________________

2. Second Most Important:

a. ________________________
b. ________________________
c. ________________________
d. ________________________
e. ________________________

3. Third Most Important:

a. ________________________
b. ________________________
c. ________________________
d. ________________________
e. ________________________

4. Fourth Most Important:

a. ____

b. ____

c. ____

d. ____

e. ____

5. Fifth Most Important:

a. ____

b. ____

c. ____

d. ____

e. ____

Now consider the barriers you might face. Barriers could include your child's interests, personality, individual strengths and weaknesses, resistance from the other parent, insufficient financial resources, or insufficient community resources. For each of your five goals, prepare a list of three to five potential barriers.

1. Most Important:

a. ____

b. ____

c. ____

d. ____

e. ____

2. Second Most Important:

a. ____

b. ____

c. ____

d. ____

e. ____

3. Third Most Important:

a. ____

b. ____

c. ____

d. ____

e. ____

4. Fourth Most Important:

a. ____

b. ____

c. ____

d. ____

e. ____

5. Fifth Most Important:

a. ____

b. ____

c. ____

d. ____

e. ____

Finally, having identified potential barriers, think about how you can work around them to achieve your goals. You may need to re-think your proposed methods. For example, if your goal is for your child to become a religious adult and their other parent refuses to allow them to attend religious school, is there a way to teach them during your own parenting time? Or if you want your child to grow up and become a confident adult, perhaps martial arts training would help. As you consider how to achieve your goals, to the extent possible, think of people other than your child's OP you can enlist to support you and your child. The purpose of this part of the activity is to decide *if* you will confront the OP with each goal and how you will do it. Or you might decide that you will **not** confront the OP about this issue and use a work-around instead. Regardless, once you have a clearly identified goal and an understanding of how the OP behaves, you can strategize your interactions with them.

PROBLEM SOLVING WITH THE OP

When the OP raises an issue, first consider whether you want to address it. Is it your problem? Will addressing it further your Personal Parenting Plan? Will addressing it reduce the OP's interference in your life? Once you have made the decision to deal with an issue, review the OP's messages (email, text messages, verbal statements) about that issue. It might help to write them down:

1. ____
2. ____
3. ____
4. ____
5. ____

Has the OP proposed any viable solutions? More importantly, if you accept their solution, what is the likely outcome? Will they follow through? What alternative solutions would you consider? Would the OP accept your recommendation *and* follow through? Prepare a list of proposed solutions. Do not say "mine" or "yours" as that will antagonize the OP. Be very matter of fact:

Problem: ____
Proposed Solution 1: ____

Proposed Solution 2: _______________________________________

Proposed Solution 3: _______________________________________

If the OP accepts one of the proposed solutions, divide up the tasks needed to achieve it. Consider taking on the more critical tasks, so you know they will be accomplished.

Finally, ask the OP if they are interested in setting up benchmarks to measure success. Be mindful that if the OP agrees, they may accuse you of failing to meet the benchmark as "they" interpret it. On the other hand, if the OP fails to meet the benchmark, you may be free to resolve the matter independently.

If the OP rejects all your proposals, have them suggest one or two more of their own. Remind them that their proposed solution should include a process for achieving success. Remember that you do not need to respond to their suggestions immediately. If you are talking in person, tell them you need to "sleep on it," and that you will get back to them. If your conversation is through email, you can say the same thing. It is important to think through the pros and cons of their proposal before agreeing, disagreeing, or attempting to tweak it so that the process for solving the problem is acceptable. If you cannot agree, then again, consider resolving the problem independently, but prepare for how you will respond to the OP's complaints.

ROLE MODELING BOUNDARIES, CRITICAL THINKING, AND PROBLEM-SOLVING, SKILLS

Once you have shored up your own emotional intelligence, role modeling boundaries should be an easy task. Simply be transparent. If you need a few minutes for yourself, perhaps to calm yourself or transition from work to home, be open and tell your child. If you find your anger becoming overwhelming, let them know that you will try to calm down. Conflicts at work or with friends or family can also teach your children how to set boundaries. Explain, in an age-appropriate way, what happened, how you responded, and why you chose that response.

The trickier situations are those involving the OP. It is not good to say that the OP did something bad and therefore you hung up the phone or walked away. It is better to tell your child that when the OP said or did something, you felt uncomfortable and thought it better to leave rather than get into an argument. This focuses the conversation on your response and not what the OP did.

When it comes to role modeling critical thinking and problem-solving, you should be more circumspect. Consider your child's age. Consider whether your child *should* be aware of the issue. For example, you do not want to ask your child why they thought the OP did or said something to *you*. That is not their concern. Nor should you ask them for help to solve *your* problems at work or with friends or family members. Rather, practice with more mundane things, such as why the grocery store raised the price of milk, or how you can be at both your son's and daughter's soccer games when they are at the same time but in separate locations. Even if your child offers irrelevant or unhelpful answers, you are inviting them to practice their critical thinking and problem-solving skills.

As your child grows and matures, the conversations will become more complex. Your older child now has relationships with family, friends, teachers, coaches, and perhaps employers. Social media has an enormous impact on young adults. Talking to them about how they responded to something they heard or that was said to them, will help them recognize their feelings. Asking why they think the other person behaved the way they did, and what your child thinks might have been done differently, helps your child critically think, problem solve, and become more self-aware.

Be open about your own thoughts and feelings with your child, in an age-appropriate way. If you have thoughts about something that happened at work, something a friend said or did, something you saw in the news or on social media, talk about it with your children. Ask them what they think. Ask what they believe prompted the event in question. What led to it? Was the response optimal or could the person have done something different? What would you do in the same situation?

These conversations can happen at the dinner table or when driving in the car. Sometimes it is good to turn off the screens and talk for a few minutes. The discussion need not be lengthy or heavy. But with repetition, your child will learn to not to accept information at face value and will become a better critical thinker and problem solver.

CREATING A CHILD CENTERED HOME

To enhance your child-centered home, think about the "perfect" family you have seen on television, in a movie, or in a book you read. Or is it a family who lives down the street that seems ideal? The crucial point to consider is what about this family appeals to you? What are the three to five adjectives you would use to describe them?

1. ____
2. ____
3. ____
4. ____
5. ____

Now think about yourself, your child, your lifestyle, and the other people in your life such as extended family and friends. Do any of those adjectives describe you and your family? If so, then consider whether you want to improve upon your existing family culture or are you happy with how your family interacts? On the other hand, if none of the adjectives describe you or your family, think about why not. Why aren't you cultivating the family life that is your ideal? Honestly list the challenges you face that prevent you from creating the family you want. In doing so, remember that the goal is not to become that "perfect" family. They are fictional. Rather, if you mindfully consider the family culture that would make you happy and have words to describe it, you can think about how you might realize it. Start by listing the barriers associated with each identified family trait:

1. Culture ____
   Barrier ____
   Barrier ____
   Barrier ____
   Barrier ____
   Barrier ____

2. Culture ____
   Barrier ____
   Barrier ____
   Barrier ____
   Barrier ____
   Barrier ____

3. Culture ____
   Barrier ____
   Barrier ____
   Barrier ____
   Barrier ____
   Barrier ____

4. Culture ____
   Barrier ____
   Barrier ____
   Barrier ____

Barrier ____

Barrier ____

5. Culture ____

Barrier ____

Barrier ____

Barrier ____

Barrier ____

Barrier ____

Consider what actions you might take to move your home life closer to the family you want. How can you remove the barriers or reshape them to be less prohibitive? Remember that perfection is not the goal. The goal is to create a home that resembles the home you had envisioned when you thought about building a family. For each goal, list the steps you might take, and finally, again, how will you measure success?

1. Behavior ____

   Steps to Change:

   a. ____

   b. ____

   c. ____

   d. ____

   e. ____

2. Behavior ____

   Steps to Change:

   a. ____

   b. ____

   c. ____

   d. ____

   e. ____

3. Behavior ____
   Steps to Change:

a. ____
b. ____
c. ____
d. ____
e. ____

4. Behavior ____
   Steps to Change:

a. ____
b. ____
c. ____
d. ____
e. ____

5. Behavior ____
   Steps to Change:

a. ____
b. ____
c. ____
d. ____
e. ____

Give yourself time. Change happens slowly and there will always be setbacks. Changing behavior is like dieting. For three days you might eat well, and on the fourth day you might have pasta and ice cream for every meal. That does not mean you should stop eating properly and carry around a bucket of chocolate candy bars with you. It does mean, you start again. And again. Until one day you look back and realize that you have made the changes you wanted to and can be proud of yourself. And then you can reward yourself with that ice cream cone or whatever it is that gives you pleasure.

BIBLIOGRAPHY

Alexa N. Joyce, High-Conflict Divorce: A form of Child Neglect, Family Court Review, Volume 54, Issue 4, October 2016, Pages 642–656.

Alberta Provincial Court. *Parenting After Separation for Families in High Conflict: Parent's Guide.* Family Mediation Program. 2014.

Amato, P. (2004, December). *Parenting through family transitions.* Social Policy Journal of New Zealand, 23, pg. 31.

American Academy of Pediatricians. (2016). *Healthy Children*; Org. https://www.healthychildren.org/English/Pages/default.aspx.

American Bar Association Family Law Section and the Johnson Foundation. (2001). *High Conflict Custody Cases: Reforming the System for Children – Conference Report and Action Plan.* Family Law Quarterly. Vol. 34. No. 4. Pg. 589.

Arizona Association of Family and Conciliation Courts. 2011. Arizona Parent Ed for High Conflict.pdf.

Arky, B. (2021). *How to Help Kids Learn to Fail,* Child Mind Institute. http://childmind.org/article/how-to-help-kids-learn-to-fail/.

Babb, B., Danziger, G., Moran, J. Englander, I. (2009). *Parent Education Programs: Review of the Literature and Annotated Bib-*

liography. Maryland Administrative Offices. Family Administration. Court Research and Development. Center for Families, Children, and the Courts. University of Baltimore School of Law.

Barnes, G. (1999, October). *Divorce Transitions: Identifying Risk and Promoting Resilience for Children and Their Parental Relationships*. Journal of Marital and Family Therapy. Vol. 4, pg. 425-441.

Baum & Shnit. (2008). *Self-Differentiation and Narcissism in Divorced Parents' Co-Parental Relationships and Functioning*, Journal of Divorce & Remarriage.

Birnbaum, R., Nicholas, B. *Towards the Differentiation of High-Conflict Families: An Analysis of Social Science Research and Canadian Law*.

Blomqvist, P., Heimer, M. (2016). *Equal Parenting when Families Break Apart: Alternative Residence and the Best Interests of the Child in Sweden*. Social Policy & Administration. Vol. 50:7, Pg. 767.

Bowles, J., Christian, K., Drew, M., Yetter, K. (2008). *A Judicial Guide to Child Safety in Custody Cases*. National Council of Juvenile and Family Court Judges.

Bricklin, B., Elliot, G. (2000). *Qualifications of and Techniques to be Used by Judges, Attorneys, and Mental Health Professionals Who Deal with Children in High Conflict Divorce Cases*. University of Arkansas at Little Rock Law Review. Vol. 22, pg. 501-897.

Carbonneau, T. (1986). *A Consideration of Alternatives to Divorce Litigation*, 1986 U. Ill. L. Rev. 1119.

Chen, J-D, George, R. (2005). *Cultivating Resilience in Children from Divorced Families*. The Family Journal: Counseling and Therapy for Couples and Families. Vol 13, No.4, pg. 452-455.

Childress, C. (2015). *Attachment-Based "Parental Alienation" A Scientifically Based Model Of "Parental Alienation.* http://drcraigchildressblog.com/.

Childress, C. (2015). *Understanding Splitting.* http://drcraigchildressblog.com/2014/09/16/key-concept-splitting/.

Cui, M., Donnellan, M. (2009, August 1). *Trajectories of Conflict over Raising Adolescent Children and Marital Satisfaction*, J Marriage Fam. 71(3): 478–494.

Czapanskiy, S. (2015). *The Shared Custody Child Support Adjustment: Not Worth the Candle.* Family Law Quarterly; Chicago. Vo. 49.3. Pg. 409.

Dalton, C., Carbon, S., Olesen, N. (2003). *High Conflict Divorce, Violence, and Abuse: Implications for Custody and Visitation Decisions.* Juvenile and Family Court Journal, Fall 2003, pg. 11.

Diagnostic and statistical manual of mental disorders: DSM-5. 5th ed. Washington,

D.C.: American Psychiatric Association, 2013

Desmond, E. (2008). *Divorce and the Family Court: What can be Done About Domestic Violence?* Family Court Review, 46:3, 531–536.

Desmond, K., Kindsvatter, A. (2013, January). *Addressing Parent-Child Conflict: Attachment-Based Interventions with Parents.* Journal of Counseling and Development. JCD91.1: 105-112.

Difonzo, J. (2015). *AFCC Think Tank Final Report on Shared Parenting: Overview, Consensus Points, and Discussion Questions.* Washington Chapter AFCC Annual Conference. Shared Parenting Predicaments: Washington's Policy and Practice Concerns.

Drodz, L., Olesen N. (2004). *Is It Abuse, Alienation, and/or Estrangement? A Decision Tree.* Journal of Child Custody. Vol. 1, Iss. 3, Pg. 65-106.

Doppler-Bourassa, E., Harkins, D., Mehta, C. (2008). *Emerging*

Empowerment: Conflict Resolution Intervention and Preschool Teachers' Reports of Conflict Behavior. Early Education and Development. Vol. 19, Iss. 6.

Elrod, L. (2001) *Reforming the System to Protect Children in High Conflict Custody.* William Mitchell Law Review. Vol. 28:2. Pg. 501.

Garber, B. (2007). *Conceptualizing Visitation Resistance and Refusal in The Context of Parental Conflict, Separation, and Divorce.* Family Court Review. Vol 45. Pg. 588.

Garber, B. (2011). *Parental Alienation and the Dynamics of the Enmeshed Parent-Child Dyad: Adultification, Parentification, and Infantilization.* Family Court Review. Vol. 49, Issue 2, Pg. 322.

Gray, P. (2015, December 22). *The Good Enough Parent Is the Best Parent.* Psychology Today. https://www.psychology today.com/blog/freedom-learn/201512/the-good-enough-parent-is-the-best-parent.

Great Schools Staff. (2009, May 27). *Self-advocacy: a valuable skill for your teenager with LD.* Great!Schools.Org. http://www.greatschools.org/gk/articles/self-advocacy-teenager-with-ld/.

Haas, T. (2004). *Child Custody Determinations in Michigan: Not in the best Interests of Children or Parents.* University of Detroit Law Review. Vol. 81:3. Pg. 334.

Hartson, J., Eau, C. (2010) *Appropriate Parenting Plans for Children Ages Zero to Two.* American Journal of Family Law. Vo. 23: Iss. 4, pg. 191.

Huntington, C. (2008). *Repairing Family Law*, 57 Duke L.J. 1245.

Inge, B. (1985). *Attachment Theory: Retrospect and Prospect.* Monographs of the Society for Research in Child Development. vol. 50, no. 1/2, 1985, pp. 3–35. www.jstor.org/stable/3333824.

Jaffe, P. (214). *A Presumption Against Shared Parenting for Family Court Litigants.* Family Court Review. Vol. 52. Pg. 187.

Johnston, J. (2005). *Children of Divorce Who Reject a Parent and Refuse Visitation: Recent Research and Social Policy Implications for The Alienated Child*. Family Law Quarterly. Vol. 38. pg. 757.

Johnston, J., Walters, M., Olesen, N. (2005). *Is It Alienation parent, Role Reversal or Child Abuse? A Study of Children's Rejection of a Parent in Child Custody Disputes*. Hawthorne Press. www.haworthpress.com.

Johnson, J., Lee, S., Olesen, N., Marjorie, W. (2005). *Allegations and Substantiations of Abuse in Custody-Disputing Families*. Family Court Review, 43:2, 283–294.

Johnston, J. (2000). *Building Multidisciplinary Professional Partnerships with the Court on Behalf of High-Conflict Divorcing Families and Their Children: Who Needs What Kind of Help?* University of Arkansas Little Rock Law Review. Vo 22. Pg. 453.

Joyce, A. (2016). *High Conflict Divorce: A Form of Child Neglect*. Family Court Review. Vol. 54. No. 4. Pg. 643.

Keng-Yen, H., Teti, D., O'Brien, M., Caughy, Feldstein, S., Genevro, J. (2007, April). *Mother-Child Conflict Interaction in the Toddler Years: Behavior Patterns and Correlates*. Journal of Child and Family Studies. Volume 16, Issue 2, pp 219–241.

Koerner, K., Linehan, M. (19__). *Dialectical Behavior Therapy for Borderline Personality Disorder*. Psychological Treatments for Severe Personality Disorders. Vol. __. Pg. 317

Kruk, E. (2015). *Co-Parenting After Divorce; What Exactly Is "The Best Interest of the Child"? The Essential Needs of Children After Parental Divorce*. Psychology Today.

Lauter, J. (2009). *Treatment With Parents in High-Conflict Divorce: An Integrative Literature Review*. Wright Institute Graduate School of Psychology.

Lee, A. (2021). *The Importance of Self-Advocacy for Kids with Learning and Attention Issues.* https://www.understood.org/en/friends-feelings/empowering-your-child/self-advocacy/the-importance-of-self-advocacy.

Levite, Z., Cohen, O. (2012). The Tango of Loving Hate: Couple Dynamics in High Conflict Divorce. Clinical Social Work Journal, 40:46-55.

Liable, D., Panfile, T., Makariev, D. (2008). *The Quality and Frequency of Mother–Toddler Conflict: Links with Attachment and Temperament,* Volume 79, Issue 2, Pages 426–443.

Linehan, M. (1993). *Skills Training Manual for Treating Borderline Personality Disorder.* The Guildford Press: New York.

Lengua, L., Wolchik, S., Braver, S. (1995). *Understanding Children's Divorce Adjustment from an Ecological Perspective.* Journal of Divorce and Remarriage. Vol. 22(3/4). Pg. 25.

McCarthy, B, Ginsbert, R. (2007). *Second Marriages: Challenges and Risks.* The Family Journal: Counseling and Therapy for Couples and Families. Vol. 15, No. 2, pg. 19-123.

McKay, B, McKay, K. (2013, October 9). *Creating a Positive Family Culture: The Importance of Establishing Family Traditions.* Family, Featured, People. http://www.artofmanliness.com/2013/10/09/creating-a-positive-family-culture-the-importance-of-establishing-family-traditions/.

Neff, R., Cooper, K. (2004). *Progress in Parent Education: Parental Conflict Resolutions: Six-, Twelve-, and Fifteen-Month Follow-Ups of a High-Conflict Program.* 42 Family Court Review 99.

Nielson, L. (2011). *Shared Parenting After Divorce: A Review of Shared Parenting Residential Parenting Research.* Journal of Divorce and Remarriage. Vol. 52. Pg. 586.

Nielsen, l. (2021) *Shared Physical Custody: Does It Benefit Most Children?* Journal of the American Academy of Matrimonial Lawyers, Vol. 28, Pg. 79. http://www.aaml.org/sites/default/files/MAT111_1.pdf.

Nehami, B., Shnit, D. (2005) *Self-Differentiation and Narcissism in Divorced Parents' Co-Parental Relationships and Functioning*, Journal of Divorce & Remarriage. Vol 42. Pg. 33

Nelson, J. (2021). *Family Meetings*. Positive Discipline. https://www.positivediscipline.com/articles/family-meetings.

NSPCC Staff. (2021). *What is Emotional Abuse?* National Society for the Prevention of Cruelty to Children. https://www.nspcc.org.uk/preventing-abuse/child-abuse-and-neglect/emotional-abuse/what-is-emotional-abuse/.

Peris, T. Emery, R. (2005) *Redefining the Parent-Child Relationship Following Divorce*, Journal of Emotional Abuse. Vol. 5 Iss. 4. Pg. 169-189.

Payson, E. (2002). *The Wizard of Oz and Other Narcissists: Coping with The One Way Relationship in Work, Love, and Family*. Julian Day Publications.

Portnoy, S. (2008). *The Psychology of Divorce: A Lawyer's Primer, part 2: The Effects of Divorce on Children*. American Journal of Family Law. Winer 21:4, pg. 126.

Prevent Child Abuse America Staff. (2021). *Emotional Abuse*. Prevent Child Abuse America. http://www.preventchildabuse.org/images/docs/emotional-childabuse.pdf.

Sarrazin, J., Cyr, F. (2007). *Parental Conflicts and Their Damaging Effects on Children*. Journal of Divorce and Remarriage. Vol 47(1/2). Pg. 77.

Schacht, T. (2000). *Prevention Strategies to Protect Professionals and Families Involved in High-Conflict Divorce*. 22 University of Arkansas at Little Rock Law Review 565.

Shure, M., Digeronimo, T., Campell, C. (Summer 1995). *Raising a Thinking Child: Help Your Child to Resolve Everyday Conflicts and Get Along with Others.* Harvard Educational Review 65.2: 339.

Stahl, P. *Parallel Parenting for High Conflict Families.* ParallelParentingForHighConflictFamilies.pdf

Sullivan, R. (2014) *The neurobiology of attachment to nurturing and abusive caregivers.* Hastings Law Journal. Vol. 63: Iss. 6, pg. 1553.

Taylor, J. (2010, March 9). *Parenting: Create a Family-value Culture; Do your children have a family-value culture to protect them?* Psychology Today.

Warshak, R. (2000), *Obstacles and controversies in the pursuit of children's best interests.* Keynote address Arizona chapter AFCC.

Warshak, R. (2014). *Securing Children's Best Interests While Resisting the Lure of Simple Solutions.* Journal of Divorce & Remarriage. Volume 56, Issue 1, pages 57-79.

Weinstein, J., Weinstein, R. (2005). *"I Know Better Than That": The Role of Emotions and the Brain.* Journal of Law and Family Studies. Vol. 7. Pg. 351.

Winnicott, DW. (1967). *Mirror-role of the mother and family in child development.* The predicament of the family: a psycho-analytical symposium. London, UK: Hogarth Press. pp. 26–33.

PRAISE FOR *WINNING YOUR HIGH-CONFLICT DIVORCE*
BY R. SHELLY LOOMUS, JD, MSW

I highly recommend this knowledgeable, thought-provoking, helpful, and realistic book written from a unique perspective. Ms. Loomus provides a comprehensive explanation to her readers with attention to detail and rich case examples to prove her points. She offers a step-by-step description of each phase of the divorcing process and anticipates every possible challenge that may be faced. Ms. Loomus shares valuable strategies, advise, and tips throughout her book. The reader will not only be well-informed but left with a sense of hope and optimism.

Toni P. Kaplan, Ph.D., Clinical Psychologist

—

I would recommend this book to anyone going through a high conflict divorce. The advice is real, and the situations are real. When you are trying to make heads or tails of a difficult ex-spouse this is a much-needed resource. It helps you see the craziness through clear lenses.

Michelle

Continued…

WINNING
YOUR HIGH-CONFLICT
DIVORCE
Strategies for Moms and Dads

R. Shelly Loomus, JD, MSW